to the new evangelization
and guide our steps along the pathways of the world,
to proclaim Christ by our lives,
and to direct our earthly pilgrimage
towards the City of heavenly light.
May Christ's followers show forth their love
for the poor and the oppressed;
may they be one with those in need
and abound in works of mercy;
may they be compassionate towards all,
that they themselves may obtain indulgence
and forgiveness from you.

Praise and glory to You, Most Holy Trinity,
you alone are God most high!

4. Father, grant that your Son's disciples,
purified in memory
and acknowledging their failings,
may be one, that the world may believe.
May dialogue between the followers
of the great religions prosper,
and may all people discover
the joy of being your children.
May the intercession of Mary,
Mother of your faithful people,
in union with the prayers of the Apostles,
the Christian martyrs,
and the righteous of all nations in every age,
make the Holy Year a time of renewed hope
and of joy in the Spirit
for each of us and for the whole Church.

Praise and glory to You, Most Holy Trinity,
you alone are God most high!

5. To you, Almighty Father,
Creator of the universe and of mankind,
through Christ, the Living One,
Lord of time and history,
in the Spirit who makes all things holy,
be praise and honour and glory
now and for ever. Amen!

4/10/2000

To Marie,
with prayerful best wishes,

+ Jam C. Timlin
Bishop of Scranton

CENTRAL COMMITTEE FOR THE GREAT JUBILEE OF THE YEAR 2000

PILGRIM PRAYERS

FOR THE JUBILEE

The Lord is my shepherd. He leads me to restore my spirit.
He guides me in paths of saving justice. Your staff is
there to comfort me. (Ps 22,1–4)
THE GOOD SHEPHERD, Mausoleum of Galla Placidia, Ravenna

CONTINUUM

CENTRAL COMMITTEE FOR THE GREAT JUBILEE OF THE YEAR 2000

EDITORIAL PROJECT AND DIRECTION
H.E. Mgr Francesco Gioia
*Member of the Central Committee
of the Great Jubilee of the Year 2000*

CELEBRATIONS AND PRAYERS
Corrado Maggioni
*Official of the Congregation for Divine Worship
and the Discipline of the Sacraments*
Consultants: Juan M. Canals, Jean Evenou
and Manlio Sodi

Reflections and Via Lucis
Gianfranco Ravasi

Image-text coordination
Crispino Valenziano

Selection of the miniatures
Giovanni Morello

Iconographic sources
La Scala Archives, Florence
Image Bank, Milan
Elemond Archives, Milan
Vatican Apostolic Library, Rome

CONTENTS

III CELEBRATIONS, PRAYERS AND SONGS

INTRODUCTION

Here is a *book of prayer* that you will find useful when you come to Rome, seat of the Pope and centre of the Catholic Church, on the occasion of the Great Jubilee of the year 2000, and also when you go back home, in your own parish.

A *book of prayer* at the beginning of the Third Millennium. After centuries and centuries of history and technological progress, people still feel the need to pray. They are absorbed by a thousand daily concerns and are often misled by the superficiality of messages around them. Yet, in spite of all this, men and women cannot do without prayer. Many are not even aware of this; others probably forget it. Yet the fact remains that the history of humankind has always been in some way intertwined with the continuous flow of prayer that rises uninterruptedly from earth to heaven. A prayer of invocation, a cry for help, a supplication, a prayer in desperation, intercession, thanksgiving, praise, silence, adoration.

The reason behind this is that the nobility of the human being, his primary significance, lies in his capacity to reach the Eternal. The human person may surround himself with all the most precious objects, achieve the greatest power, enjoy all earthly pleasures, but in him, there will always be a void that only God can fill.

However, unlike other religions, the Christian faith affirms that union with God is achieved not by leaving the world but, on the contrary, by being deeply rooted in it. Think of Jerusalem, Rome, Lourdes, Fatima, Loreto, Pompeii, Guadalupe, San Giovanni Rotondo, Czestochowa, Mariazell, Aparecida, Lujan, Santiago de Compostela, Assisi, Mount Athos and other countless places of pilgrimage. Christianity loves the world, although it dramatically knows that the world despises and persecutes it.

Praying in Rome means being united with God and with the Church. It means raising our eyes to heaven and giving our hand to our brothers and sisters. It means celebrating the only One who is Absolute and acknowledging that we are guided by the Magisterium of the Church.

May your prayer at the Eternal City always accompany you in your daily life, far from the Eternal City but constantly united with the Church, my sister and my brother in the faith in Jesus Christ!

Cardinal Roger Etchegaray

Preface

The pilgrims who come to Rome for the Great Jubilee of the Year 2000 will wish to be "accompanied" during their visit to the holy places in order to better understand their religious significance and worthily live their encounter with our Saviour.

The Secretariat of the Central Committee for the Great Jubilee instituted a Commission* charged with the task of preparing two appropriate publications: a guide-book, *Pilgrims in Rome*, to help pilgrims enjoy the Christian significance of the Eternal City, and a collection of texts, *Pilgrim Prayers*, for group and personal prayer and meditation. Although they are distinct from each other, the two books are complementary. The guide-book stresses the spiritual message inherent in each holy place, which the prayer book develops in expressions of prayer.

As well as the meditations and celebrations connected with the holy places, *Pilgrim Prayers* offers texts that foster moments of group and personal prayer and reflection. Along with the liturgical celebrations, ample space is given to some acts of piety that are dear to Christian people.

The pictures, a witness of the Christian faith expressed in all kinds of art in two millennia of history, are not simply illustrations. According to the liturgical tradition of the Church, they complete the text of a prayer by offering to the eyes what the words offer to the ears, clearly revealing the grace of the mysteries of our Saviour and exalting, through their colours, the beauty of Mary and the saints.

These books are also a valid aid to the individual local Churches, called to organize specific moments of celebration and prayer during the jubilee year. You are invited to adapt the celebrations suggested for specific holy places in the city of Rome to the needs of your own situation. This could be done by choosing churches that are linked with the themes of the celebrations.

I hope that this precious collection of prayers will help you feel that you are a living part of the Church which, in the name of Christ, is crossing the threshold of the Third Millennium.

H.E. Mgr Crescenzio Sepe

*Members of the Commission: H.E. Mgr Francesco Gioia (President), Ferdinando Belli (Secretary), Carlo Chenis, Antonio Collicelli, Nicolò Costa, Carmelo Dotolo, Raffaella Giuliani, Corrado Maggioni, Luca Mariani, Francesco Marinelli, Danilo Mazzoleni, Mario Sensi.

I
THE MEANING
OF THE JUBILEE

You will sound the trumpet-call.
You will declare this fiftieth year to be sacred
and proclaim liberation. (Lev 25, 9–10)
THE SOUND OF THE SHOFAR, Israel Museum, Jerusalem

I NCARNATIONIS MYSTERIUM

Bull of Indiction

With the Bull Incarnationis Mysterium *Pope John Paul II proclaimed the Holy Year of 2000. In it, he described the spirit that should animate the event and the signs that should denote it.*

Here are the salient passages of sections 7–13.

In the course of its history, the institution of the Jubilee has been enriched by signs which attest to the faith and foster the devotion of the Christian people. Among these, the first is the notion of *pilgrimage*, which is linked to the situation of man, who readily describes his life as a journey. From birth to death, the condition of each individual is that of the *homo viator* … It evokes the believer's personal journey in the footsteps of the Redeemer: it is an exercise of practical asceticism, of repentance for human weaknesses, of constant vigilance over one's own frailty, of interior preparation for a change of heart.

In addition to pilgrimage, there is the sign of the *holy door*. It evokes the passage from sin to grace which every Christian is called to accomplish. Jesus said: "I am the door" (Jn 10, 7), in order to make it clear that no one can come to the Father except through him … Through the holy door, symbolically more spacious at the end of a millennium, Christ will lead us more deeply into the Church, his Body and his Bride.

Another distinctive sign is the *indulgence*, which is one of the constitutive elements of the Jubilee. The indulgence discloses the fullness of the Father's mercy, who offers everyone his love, expressed primarily in the forgiveness of sins ... With the indulgence, the repentant sinner receives a remission of the temporal punishment due for the sins already forgiven as regards the fault. Nor will the People of God fail to recognize other possible signs of the mercy of God at work in the Jubilee. First of all, the sign of the *purification of memory*; this calls everyone to make an act of courage and humility in recognizing the wrongs done by those who have borne or bear the name of Christian. By its nature, the Holy Year is a time when we are called to conversion ... As the Successor of Peter, I ask that in this year of mercy the Church, strong in the holiness which she receives from her Lord, should kneel before God and implore forgiveness for the past and present sins of her sons and daughters.

One sign of the mercy of God which is especially necessary today is the sign of *charity*, which opens our eyes to the needs of those who are poor and excluded. Such is the situation affecting vast sectors of society and casting its shadow of death upon whole peoples ... The Jubilee is a further summons to conversion of heart through a change of life. It is a reminder to all that they should give absolute importance neither to the goods of the earth, since these are not God, nor to humanity's domination or claim to domination, since the earth belongs to God and to God alone.

A sign of the truth of Christian love, ageless but especially powerful today, is the memory of the martyrs. Their witness must not be forgotten. They are the ones who have proclaimed the Gospel by giving their lives for love. The martyr, especially in our own days, is a sign of that greater love which sums up all other values.

Conditions for the Jubilee Indulgence

All the faithful, properly prepared, can fully enjoy throughout the Jubilee, the gift of the indulgence, in accordance with the following norms.

While indulgences granted either generally or by special rescript remain in force during the Great Jubilee, it should be noted that the Jubilee indulgence also can be applied in suffrage to the souls of the deceased: such an offering constitutes an outstanding act of supernatural charity, in virtue of the bond which, in the Mystical Body of Christ, unites the faithful still on pilgrimage here below and those who have already ended their earthly journey. Then too, the rule that a plenary indulgence can be gained only once a day remains in force during the entire Jubilee year.

The high point of the Jubilee is the encounter with God the Father, through Christ the Saviour present in his Church and in a special way in the Sacraments. For this reason, the whole Jubilee journey, prepared for by pilgrimage, has as its starting point and its conclusion the celebration of the Sacraments of Penance and of the Eucharist, the paschal mystery of Christ, our peace and our reconciliation: this is the transforming encounter which opens us to the gift of the indulgence for ourselves and for others.

After worthily celebrating sacramental confession, which ordinarily, according to the norm of Canon 960 of the Code of Canon Law and of Canon 720 § 1 of the Code of Canons of the Eastern Churches, must be individual and complete, each member of the faithful, having fulfilled the required conditions, can receive or apply the gift of the plenary indulgence during a suitable period of time, even daily, without needing to go to confession again. It is fitting however that the faithful should frequently receive the grace of the Sacrament of Penance, in order to grow in conversion and in purity of heart. Participation in the Eucharist, which is required for all indulgences, should properly take place on the same day as the prescribed works are performed.

These two culminating moments must be accompanied, first of all, by the witness of communion with the Church, manifested by prayer for the intentions of the Roman Pontiff, and also by acts of charity and penance, following the indications given below: these acts are meant to express the true conversion of heart to which communion with Christ in the Sacraments leads. Christ is truly our forgiveness and the expiation of our sins (cf. 1 Jn 2, 2). By pouring into the hearts of the faithful the Holy Spirit who is the "remission of all sins", he guides each individual towards a filial and trusting encounter with the Father of mercies. From this encounter springs a commitment to conversion and renewal, to ecclesial communion and to charity towards our brothers and sisters. Likewise confirmed for the Jubilee is the norm whereby confessors can commute, on behalf of those legitimately impeded, both the work prescribed and the conditions required. Cloistered men and women religious, the infirm and all those who for whatever reason are not able to leave their own house, can carry out, in lieu of a visit to a certain Church, a visit to the chapel of their house; should even this be impossible for them, they can gain the indulgence by spiritually uniting themselves with those carrying out the prescribed work in the ordinary manner and by offering to God their prayers, sufferings and discomforts. With regard to the required conditions, the faithful can gain the Jubilee indulgence:

1) *In Rome*, if they make a pious pilgrimage to one of the Patriarchal Basilicas, namely, the Basilica of Saint Peter in the Vatican, the Archbasilica of the Most Holy Saviour at the Lateran, the Basilica of Santa Maria Maggiore and the Basilica of Saint Paul on the Ostian Way, and there take part devoutly in Holy Mass or another liturgical celebration such as Lauds or Vespers, or some pious exercise (e.g., the Stations of the Cross, the Rosary, the recitation of the *Akathistos* Hymn in honour of the Mother of God); furthermore, if they visit, as a group or individually, one of the four Patriarchal Basilicas and

...cal

...he poor: "It will

...nd. But what the land produces in

...ie, your employee and your guest residing with you" ...rve to feed you, your slave, male or

(cf. 25, 1-7). Further ahead, it fixed a jubilee year, the fiftieth

after seven weeks of years: "You will keep this as a jubilee"

(Lev 25, 10). This, too, is a year of the remission of debts and

the liberation of slaves (cf. Lev 25, 4-17). Hence, there are

three steps. A sabbatical year for the land and of the remis-

there spend some time in Eucharistic adoration and pious meditations, ending with the Our Father, the profession of faith in any approved form, and prayer to the Blessed Virgin Mary. To the four Patriarchal Basilicas are added, on this special occasion of the Great Jubilee, the following further places, under the same conditions: the Basilica of Santa Croce in Gerusalemme, the Basilica of Saint Lawrence in Campo Verano, the Shrine of Our Lady of Divine Love, and the Christian Catacombs.

2) In the Holy Land, if, in keeping the same conditions, they visit the Basilica of the Holy Sepulchre in Jerusalem, or the Basilica of the Nativity in Bethlehem or the Basilica of the Annunciation in Nazareth.

3) In other ecclesiastical territories, if they make a sacred pilgrimage to the Cathedral Church or to other Churches or places designated by the Ordinary, and there assist devoutly at a liturgical celebration, or other pious exercise, such as those mentioned above for the City of Rome; in addition, if they visit, in a group or individually, the Cathedral Church or a Shrine designated by the Ordinary, and there spend some time in pious meditation, ending with the Our Father, the profession of faith in any approved form, and prayer to the Blessed Virgin Mary.

4) In any place, if they visit for a suitable time their brothers and sisters in need or in difficulty (the sick, the imprisoned, the elderly living alone, the handicapped, etc.), as if making a pilgrimage to Christ present in them (cf. Mt 25, 34–36), and fulfilling the usual spiritual and sacramental conditions and saying the usual prayers. The faithful will certainly wish to repeat these visits throughout the Holy Year, since on each occasion they can gain the plenary indulgence, although obviously not more than once a day.

The plenary indulgence of the Jubilee can also be gained through actions which express in a practical and generous way the penitential spirit which is, as it were, the heart of the Jubilee. This would include abstaining for at least one whole day from unnecessary consumption

and de...
supporting by a significant co...
gious or social nature (especially for...
doned children, young people in trouble, the... better
need, immigrants in various countries seeking... personal
living conditions); devoting a suitable portion of personal
free time to activities benefiting the community, or other
similar forms of personal sacrifice.

(Decree issued 29 November 1998 by the Apostolic Penitentiary and annexed to the Bull Incarnationis Mysterium*)*

And forgive us our debts: by your ineffable mercy, by virtue of the passion of your Son and through the intercession and merits of the Most Blessed Virgin Mary and all your saints
(Francis of Assisi)
PORTRAIT OF SAINT FRANCIS, Cimabue, Lower Basilica, Assisi

(e.g., from smoking or alcohol, or fasting or practising abstinence according to the general rules of the Church and the norms laid down by the Bishops' Conferences) donating a proportionate sum of money to the poor; contribution works of a reli- the benefit of aban- the elderly in

PSE EST IUBILEUS (Lev 25,10)

You will keep this as a jubilee

As the first action in his ministry, Jesus presented himself to his fellow-villagers, in Nazareth, the village where he grew up, during a ceremony at the synagogue (Lk 4, 14–30). A modest scene for a transcendental action. Luke wrote his narrative in the form of a programmatic synthesis of a message, its acceptance and rejection.

"All eyes in the synagogue were fixed on him" (v. 20). With surprising simplicity, Jesus announced that the great jubilee had come. Not one among many, but the definitive one, inaugurating the messianic period: "a year of favour from the Lord" (v. 19). To announce his own personal jubilee, Jesus made use of a prophecy of the book of Isaiah (Is 61, 1–4). The prophet was presented as one anointed by the "spirit of the Lord", invested with power and charged with the proclamation of a message of liberation. To those who suffer oppression and misery, he proclaimed not a traditional jubilee but an extraordinary intervention of God. When Jesus took possession of the oracle, the fulfilment of the proclamation began. It was a historical moment, with specific characteristics: "This text is being fulfilled today even while you are listening." The text of Isaiah 61 is based on the legislation of Deuteronomy, chapter 15, which determined a seventh year, a holy year, of the remission of debts and setting slaves free. Leviticus furthermore fixed a sabbatical year of fallow in favour of the land and of the ... be a year of rest for the la... its Sabbath will se... fem...

Praise him with the clamour of cymbals,
praise him with triumphant cymbals. (Ps 150, 5)
CHOIR, L. Della Robbia, Museo dell'Opera del Duomo, Florence

sion of debts, every seven years, and a jubilee year every fifty years. The third is a prophesied period, not defined as to duration or periodicity, with a broader content.

Have the laws and prophecy been fulfilled? As far as we can see, they have remained a humanitarian ideal in Israel. Prophecy has been left uncertain. Jesus came to accomplish the content of the laws and prophecy: a jubilee era of remission, of grace, of freedom. Not a year, but an era, in which we live and go on living.

We celebrate periodical jubilees to encourage ourselves to fulfil the contents and the demands of the jubilee. What does the jubilee ask of us? First of all, to be like those who were listening to him in Nazareth and keep our eyes "fixed on him", because it is the jubilee of our Lord Jesus Christ. It was he who proclaimed it. We actualize it as follows: *good news to the afflicted*, translated into effective help; liberty to captives: from their vices and from the cruelty of others; *sight to the blind*: corporal and spiritual, healing of other deficiencies; *freedom to the oppressed*: by greed, by ambition, by egoism, by fear; *year of grace*: remission of faults and sins, as well as of international debt.

Show unto us the blessed fruit of thy womb, Jesus.
O sweet Virgin Mary! (Hail Sant'Agostino, Holy Queen)
Madonna of the Pilgrims, Caravaggio, Saint Augustine, Rome

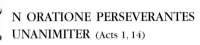

N ORATIONE PERSEVERANTES UNANIMITER (Acts 1, 14)

With one heart joined constantly in prayer

The authentic spirit of the Holy Year brings a rediscovery of Christian prayer. The proof of the sincerity of prayer is the renewal of life. For Jesus' disciples, praying means travelling on this earth doing the will of the Father who is in heaven. Christian prayer, in fact, is always generated by the Word of God. It is connected with the mysteries of the life of Jesus, a source of ecclesial communion, and filled with concrete commitments. In line with this, the Jubilee practices acquire meaning if they are anchored in the economy of the sacraments. The spiritual dynamic of the Jubilee is rooted in the sacraments of Penance and the Eucharist.

The Bull of Pope Boniface VIII for the Jubilee of 1300 recalled the remission of the punishment to reconciled penitents who visited the Basilicas of Saint Peter and of Saint Paul. In the Letter *Tertio Millennio Adveniente*, Pope John Paul II indicated the year 2000 as a year of thanksgiving, expressed through the Holy Eucharist. The years of preparation helped rediscover the sacraments of Baptism (1997), Confirmation (1998) and Penance (1999). The prayer of the Holy Year is first and foremost the confirmation and the internalization of the various elements of the liturgical prayer of the Church.

The Jubilee period opens with the joyous opening of the holy door. Not just the shutters are opened. Walls are broken down, almost with the aim of getting a new passageway. It is a visible expression of the interior act of removing the obstacles that are responsible for hindering the encounter with God. He has in fact been revealed to all men and women by Jesus Christ, the Way and the Gate of access to communion with the Father (cf. Jn 14, 6; 10, 7–9).

From the year 1500, the ceremonies accompanying the opening of the holy door have been handed down from generation to generation. During this celebration, the Pope crosses the holy door as Psalm 100 is sung: "Praise the Lord, all the earth, serve the Lord with gladness, come into his presence with songs of joy! ... Come within his gates giving thanks, to his courts singing praise, give thanks to him and bless his name!" (vv. 1–2,4). Jesus said: "I am the gate of the sheepfold ... Anyone who enters through me will be safe" (Jn 10, 7–9). Considered in the light of this affirmation, *the passage through the holy door* has the symbolic power of recalling the desire to fathom more profoundly and with a purified heart, the mystery of Jesus Christ and of the Church, which is his body.

Visiting the four major Basilicas of the city of Rome prolongs the pilgrimage so that pilgrims may achieve and preserve the interior disposition necessary for an encounter with God and with their brothers and sisters. These visits also signify a physical contact with the Church of Rome in order to obtain its spiritual fruit. It is the mission of the Bishop of Rome to preside over the communion of the universal Church.

One of the Jubilee practices is the *recitation of the Creed.* The faith professed through our lips must also be translated into a life of faith. Living as believers is the pledge that we confirm at the tombs of the Apostles. Walking in a new life corresponds to living the grace and the commitment of being "children of God". *Praying the Our Father* expresses a filial conversion to God the Father. At the same time, it makes us acknowledge others as our brothers and sisters, who are ready to be educated to divine forgiveness ("forgive us our trespasses as we forgive those who trespass against us"), happy to live in the "deliverance from evil" granted to us in Baptism and continuously revitalized through Penance and the fruitful participation in the Eucharist.

Like the Apostles, the followers of Christ must be "with one heart joined constantly in prayer" (Acts 1, 14).

RANGE ESURIENTI PANEM TUUM (Is 58, 7)

Share your bread with the poor

The Jubilee is illuminated by the year of grace proclaimed by the prophet Isaiah and announced by Jesus Christ at the beginning of his public ministry. It is the time "to bring the good news to the afflicted, to proclaim liberty to captives, sight to the blind, to let the oppressed go free" (Lk 4, 18). In participating in the Jubilee celebrations, it is necessary "to lay greater emphasis on the Church's preferential option for the poor and the outcast" (TMA 51). Christ lives in the poor. The New Testament encourages us to recognize Christ in the poor and the poor in Christ, by serving him in them. This was done by saints of all centuries and in all countries. They spent their lives for their neighbours in need.

The needs of the poor have many aspects, both corporal and spiritual. They are hungry for food and clothing, but also for a meaning in life. The Christian community, therefore, should not just be concerned with material needs, however important they may be, but also share with the poor a living faith, full of joy and hope. Every day, we see whole nations crucified, but it is easy to forget them. Often, political decisions, economic structures, or deeply rooted cultural attitudes relegate the poor to permanent poverty. In addition to material aid, the Church knows that she can and must give a word of hope. That word is Christ: he won a victory over evil that compels human beings to live in moral misery, over sin that makes them close their heart in egoism, over the fear of death that threatens them. The challenge that we face is to recognize the disfigured and crucified Lord in the crucified nations and to awaken consciences at the sight of their deplorable situation. Contemplation of the crucified Lord cannot simply remain a devotional exercise, nor can it end in meditating on a past event. The Lord lives in his members, especially in the poor. The call of the great Jubilee is to see him and serve him precisely there in them.

True Christian love is concrete. Love put into practice is much more difficult than love in dreams. As the New Testament states, true love is not only *affective*, but also *effective*. It requires the disposition of a servant. Servants work hard for a long time. They dirty their hands. They are at the frontline in serving the poor, in "sharing (their) food with the hungry" (Is 58, 7). Being open to the needs of our brothers and sisters implies sincere welcome, which is possible only if evangelical poverty is part of our personal conviction.

The Church of the poor therefore proclaims the Jubilee through the *language of acts* of justice and mercy, signs of the presence of the Kingdom of God in our midst.

Through the *language of words*: a profoundly convinced proclamation of the presence of the Lord, his love, his offer of mercy and universal welcome.

Through the *language of relationships*: being with the poor, forging bonds of friendship, forming a community that will reveal the love of the Lord for everyone. The Jubilee of the year 2000 challenges the Church to be creative in celebrating the event *with* and *for* the poor.

PEREGRINI ET HOSPITES SUPRA TERRAM
(Heb 11, 13)

Pilgrims and strangers on earth

A pilgrim on the way to a homeland or an aimless wanderer? The direct evidence of common destiny would lead us to believe that living means being hurled towards death. Life would be nothing else but a long journey towards darkness, which everyone foresees as the last shore, absolute silence. This is why it is mixed with suffering. Yet, it is for this reason that the human person poses questions. If death did not exist, with all the expressions of suffering that come with it, one would not be anxious to ask questions nor experience the thirst to discover. It is suffering that provokes us to ask, making the need for a meaning a question for all.

Thus, suffering reveals life to itself, more strongly than death which produces it, because it teaches that we are not simply hurled towards death but that in our most profound being, we are called to life. The two travellers along the road to Emmaus were oppressed by the hardness of the events in which death seemed to have conquered the life which is the source of every life (cf. Lk 24). In the same way, the inhabitants of time know the universal experience of suffering, which seems to interrupt every dream of victory over death.

The Stranger who came up and walked by their side did not stop their grief. Instead, he let them take the hurt in their soul seriously, without fleeing or getting confused before the tragedy of death. When we think of death, a miracle takes place. Living will no longer be just learning how to die, but a struggle to give meaning to life. It is there, where the question comes from, where one does not surrender before death, that the dignity and the beauty of existence are revealed: "Was it not necessary that Christ should suffer before entering into his glory?" (Lk 24, 26)

Between longing and hope, the human being is a searcher for the distant home: "Did not our hearts burn within us as he talked to us on the road and explained the scriptures to us?" (Lk 24, 32). If the human person is a pilgrim towards life, a beggar of heaven, then feeling successful, being exiles in this world no longer, becomes a mortal temptation.

Salvation is accomplished when night is acknowledged as night and there is a thirst for a word of light to brighten the impending darkness: "They pressed him to stay with them saying, 'It is nearly evening, and the day is almost over," (Lk 24, 29). To this eagerness, that transformed grieving wanderers into pilgrims of hope, Christ responded with the gift of his presence: "While he was with them at table, he took the bread and said the blessing; then he broke it and handed it to them. And their eyes were opened and they recognized him" (Lk 24, 30–31). Christ is the pilgrim who came from the Eternal to call human persons to the liberty of becoming pilgrims towards the Eternal over and over again. *Thus, pilgrimages become an icon of life*: We are "only pilgrims and strangers on earth" (Heb 11, 13). The human person is in exodus, permanently called to go out of himself, to question himself, to search for a home. A metaphor of life, the pilgrimage becomes an anticipation of the world that is to come, a pledge of the feast of the Kingdom, a renewed experience of the encounter that changes the heart. This is because it reveals God who illumines the things that have passed, gives value to the present and allows a foretaste of the ultimate and future promises, and makes him loved. Let us stay pilgrims in the night, but joyfully standing on the word of the promise that came forth from Silence, anxious before the question that can shake any easily found certainty of faith. "When the Son of Man comes, will he find any faith on earth?" (Lk 18, 8). Along this way, we shall be pilgrims directed towards the encounter with the Eternal, who came to dwell in and redeem time. We shall be pilgrims clinging to the Word, echoing the word "Maranatha", an invocation, a yearning, an expectation: "Come, Lord!"

*Two of them were on their way
to a village called Emmaus* (Lk 24, 13)
Towards Emmaus, Duccio, Sienna Cathedral

IC TE OPORTET ET ROMAE TESTIFICARI (Acts 23, 11)

*Now you must bear
witness for me in Rome*

A pilgrimage to Rome on the occasion of the Great Jubilee of the year 2000 is a spiritual experience that could be very much richer if pilgrims were aware of its significance.

It allows them to know more profoundly the *meaning of the Church*. In fact, Rome is marked by the martyrdom of the princes of the Apostles, Peter and Paul. Jesus expressly told Paul: "Now you must bear witness for me in Rome" (Acts 23, 11). The Church that is in Rome, which Paul already addressed in his letter in the years 57–58, has Peter as its Bishop. His mission to the universal Church continues in his successors. The meaning of Peter's ministry, a ministry of unity and truth, has always been perceived since the very beginning. Evidence of this awareness, which became explicit in later centuries, was already present among the very first Christian generations. Sometime around 110–130, Ignatius of Antioch affirmed, in his *Letter to the Romans*, that the Church of Rome "presides over the communion of charity". Towards 202, Irenaeus of Lyons spoke of the Church "founded and constituted in Rome by the glorious Apostles Peter and Paul", to whom the Church's tradition is bound. "For with the Church of Rome on account of its more effective leadership every Church must agree, that is, the faithful throughout the world, in which the apostolic tradition has always been preserved by the faithful everywhere" (*Adversus haereses*, III.3).

Pilgrimage in the heart of Christianity also includes visits to the monuments that marked the history of

Christian devotion: cemeteries, churches and basilicas that constitute a unique artistic inheritance.

The names of the popes that have contributed to the growth and vitality of the liturgical life of the Church, guide pilgrims through the history of Christian prayer. Certainly, the history of the popes is a tormented one and includes shadows. In some periods, intrigues and political factors cast dark clouds on the exercise of Peter's ministry.

But the history of the Church of Rome is first and foremost a history of holiness: the martyrdom of Peter and Paul was to be followed by that of other witnesses.

Men and women saints, who were born, lived and ended their earthly life in Rome, are numerous. Also numerous are those who, guided by the secure instinct of faith, felt the need to become pilgrims to Peter's Chair.

In his encyclical Letter *Ut unum sint* (1995), Pope John Paul II offered a moving meditation on the exercise and the spirituality of his mission. That meditation can dissipate the mist that obscures our sight: "It is important to note how the weakness of Peter and Paul clearly shows that the Church is founded upon the infinite power of grace" (no. 91).

"As heir to the mission of Peter in the Church, which has been made fruitful by the blood of the Princes of the Apostles, the Bishop of Rome exercises a ministry originating in the manifold mercy of God. This mercy converts hearts and pours forth the power of grace where the disciple experiences the bitter taste of his personal weakness and helplessness.

"The authority proper to this ministry is completely at the service of God's merciful plan and it must always be seen in this perspective. Its power is explained from this perspective" (no. 92). The meaning of unity and of catholicity is a gift of God, which we must pray for especially during the Jubilee.

BI ERAT MATER IESU (Jn 2, 1)

The mother of Jesus was there

Like many pilgrims today, Mary – according to the Gospel of Luke (1, 39–56) – took a long journey through the mountains, not put off by possible dangers, without waiting for others to accompany her, without any special protection.

She kept the secret of a presence that delighted her, for which the entire nation was waiting, but which no one imagined was hidden there, in the virgin womb of a woman who belonged to the common people. Her pilgrimage along the roads of Israel was the breakthrough of the new creation. When she reached the house of Elizabeth, she felt that a new relationship with her cousin was born. She knew she could reveal the mystery that was enfolding her. In humility, she sang the Magnificat, happy to have cooperated in the pact of reconciliation between heaven and earth. The grace that was poured upon her passed to Elizabeth. She is the figure of all those to whom Mary transmitted her gift, producing in them a complete transformation, as happened to John in his mother's womb.

The Jubilee will not achieve its aim if this celebration of the Incarnation does not help us discover that Mary is beside us, "the mother of Jesus is there" (Jn 2, 1). We have the example of the disciple who, at the foot of the Cross, "took her into his home" (Jn 19, 27). Extraordinary people like Joseph and John are not afraid to take Mary "with them". A person cannot welcome Mary into his or her home without adopting the code of love that means sacrifice. Often, however, when Christians live together, their spirit can tend towards mediocrity. They can become Sunday Christians. Habitual activity can turn religious men and women into professionals. Life together can generate envy, frustration, persecution within Christian families and within the walls of the convent. Christians can lack the direct, simple, spiritual and profound mode of conversation that existed between Mary and Elizabeth. The Jubilee is a precious occasion to renew this spiritual life of joy in communion, to renew the community that Jesus created.

Elizabeth, informed by the Spirit, knew the identity of the person before her. She blessed her little but great relative, echoing the greeting of the angel, which would later on be repeated *ad infinitum* by all Christians. "Of all women you are the most blessed, and blessed is the fruit of your womb" (Lk 1, 42).

The Jubilee is an occasion to rejoice with Mary for God's surprises, for his "great things", paradoxes that only little ones or saints are able to understand.

Why should I be honoured with a visit from the mother of my Lord? (Lk 1, 43)
CISTERCIAN GRADUAL, Karlsruhe, Germany

MNE DEBITUM DIMISI TIBI
(Mt 18, 32)

I cancelled all that debt of yours

Indulgence, i.e. the cancellation of "all that debt" (Mt 18, 32) contracted by sin, is an integral part of the celebration of the Holy Year. Together, let us try to understand its meaning, in the light of the *Catechism of the Catholic Church* (CCC nos. 1471–1497).

The punishments of sin. Our sins have two consequences: guilt and punishment. Because of my sin I am guilty before God (cf. nos. 1849–1851). However, my sins have lasting consequences, too. I have caused damage, to myself and to others, which must be repaired. An authentic repentance, the confession of sins and sacramental absolution through the priest immediately obtain God's complete forgiveness of my guilt. However, my obligation to accept its consequences and just punishment remains. Thus, every sin needs not only to be forgiven but also to be purified "either here on earth, or after death in the state called Purgatory" (no. 1472).

The *communion of saints.* "No man is an island." We are linked to one another like communicating vessels. Through my sins, I injure everybody else. But, thanks be to God, the good that I am able to accomplish is spread to everybody else much more than evil (cf. no. 1475). Christ "is the sacrifice to expiate our sins, and not only ours, but also those of the whole world" (1 Jn 2, 2). But whoever lived and died with him and for him, and because of this brings his redeeming love to all men and women, is a help to us. Mary and all the saints help us carry our burden, relieve us and welcome us into the great and saving family of God.

The *treasure of the Church.* It consists in the in-

O Trinity most high! Turn your merciful eye on your creatures. I run and cry before your mercy so that you may have mercy on the world (Catherine of Sienna)

MONUMENT IN HONOUR OF SAINT CATHERINE OF SIENNA, F. Messina, Rome

finite and inexhaustible value that the life and love, the sacrifice on the cross and the resurrection of Jesus Christ have for all men and women of all times. He himself is the immense and precious treasure of the Church: "From his fullness we have, all of us, received – one gift replacing another" (Jn 1, 16). The indulgence signifies that the Church, body and bride of Christ (cf. CCC no. 796), which is most closely bound to him, has the faculty to communicate and spread this fullness of grace. After all, the Lord himself conferred on her the power to bind and to loose (cf. Mt 16, 19), so that his redeeming grace would be open to all. The Church therefore gives indulgences on special occasions to offer an aid, with the grace of Christ and the merits of the saints, in the journey of repentance and sanctification.

Thus, how should the gift of the indulgence be received? Through the indulgence, the Church reminds us that we need not only the remission of our sins, but also the reparation of their consequences. She guides us to live in fullness in the communion of saints and strengthens our trust in the help of Christ and the saints, thus urging us to be a blessing for our brothers and sisters. She teaches us to realize that being the bride of Christ, she can totally reach into her fullness for us, especially in the year of the Jubilee.

II
THE "STATIONS"
OF PRAYER

I rejoiced when I heard them say:
"Let us go to God's house."
And now our feet are standing
within your gates, O Jerusalem. (Ps 121, 1)
THE HEAVENLY JERUSALEM,
Triumphal Arch, Santa Maria Maggiore, Rome

SAINT PETER'S BASILICA

*This celebration,
having as a theme the Church
"the way to Christ",
can take place,
adapted as necessary,
in the cathedral of the diocese.*

*"Lord", Peter cried, "save me!"
Jesus put out his hand at once
and held him* (Mt 14, 30–31)
"La Navicella", School of Giotto,
Saint Peter's, Rome

UPER HANC PETRAM (Mt 16, 18)

On the rock of Peter

Reflection

"The history of the Church is the living account of an unfinished pilgrimage. To journey to the city of Saints Peter and Paul, to the Holy Land, or to the old and new shrines dedicated to the Virgin Mary and the Saints: this is the goal of countless members of the faithful who find nourishment for their devotion in this way" (IM, 7). The pilgrimage, as the Bull of Indiction suggests, has as one of its main reference points the figure of the Apostle Peter. His name appears 154 times in the New Testament; other times it appears as Simon, which is his original name, while nine times it is reported as Cephas, in Aramaic. With so many references, one can even trace out a biographical sketch of the man.

Within the Gospels we have the story of a fisherman, suddenly faced with the call from Jesus on the shore of the sea of Tiberias.

We also know something about his mother-in-law who was healed from fever by Jesus; we often see him by the side of his master on the roads of Galilee, Samaria and Judaea.

We notice him on the mountain during the transfiguration, surrounded by the light of that unique manifestation. He is also present at that decisive moment when, in northern Galilee, at Caesarea Philippi, Jesus proclaims those surprising words: "You are Peter, and on this rock I will build my church" (Mt 16, 18).

In the New Testament the symbol of the rock is only used in reference to Jesus and to Peter: a symbol which in the Old Testament is reserved for God as the source of hope and security for the believer.

Christians have in Christ their perfect foundation stone (1 Cor 3, 11) while Peter has the role of making visible this solid hope which can weather any storm and is not afraid of death: around Peter "the rock", Christians find stability and unity in Christ.

Those keys and that power "to bind and to loose" represent the mission of Peter the solid rock where peace is found in the forgiveness of sins, the word of life and participation in God's Kingdom.

Peter's personal story is that of the disciple who is conscious of his own shortcomings. The betrayal during that night when Jesus gave himself up for us, makes him very much one of us, able to understand our weaknesses.

But it also transforms him into an example to be followed when, on the shore of that lake which first saw him as a fisherman, he meets the risen Christ who asks him: "Simon, son of John, do you love me more than these others do?", and Peter gives an answer which is intense and simple at the same time: "Lord, you know everything; you know I love you" (Jn 21, 15.17).

Thus, Peter returns to be fully the shepherd of the Church who has the role of "strengthening his brothers in faith" (Lk 22, 32), giving witness – even through his successors – to the solid rock of Christ which in him is proclaimed to the world, a testimony in the midst of the changing scene of the world and the weaknesses which are part of our nature.

In fact, in his first letter he wrote: "Come to him, to that living stone, rejected by men but in God's sight chosen and precious; and like living stones be yourselves built into a spiritual house" (1 Pet 2, 4–5). On his tomb in Rome, which is a seal on his human story, there is found the sign of the continuity of the Church of Christ. Christianity is on a pilgrimage to find the solid rock of faith, but also to renew that hope of which Peter wrote: "And when the chief shepherd appears, you will be given the unfading crown of glory" (1 Pet 5, 4).

I will give you the keys of the Kingdom of Heaven (Mt 16, 19)
Pilgrims' kisses have worn away the foot of this bronze statue
Bronze statue of Saint Peter Arnolfo di Cambio, Saint Peter's Rome

APUT CORPORIS
ECCLESIAE (Col 1, 18)

The Church the Body of Christ

Celebration

Towards the Basilica

The pilgrims are gathered outside the church. The animator leads the prayer with Psalm 100:

℟ Come let us adore Christ
   King and Lord of the Apostles.

Cry out with joy to the Lord, all the earth.
Serve the Lord with gladness.
Come before him, singing for joy. ℟

Know that he, the Lord, is God.
He made us, we belong to him,
we are his people, the sheep of his flock. ℟

Go within his gates, giving thanks.
Enter his courts with songs of praise.
Give thanks to him and bless his name. ℟

Indeed, how good is the Lord,
eternal his merciful love.
He is faithful from age to age. ℟

Glory. ℟

The animator recalls the meaning of going through the Holy Door and the visit to the tomb of Peter:

While approaching the signs of the presence of Christ, let us prepare ourselves with a spirit of faith: He is the Door who introduces us to the Father, the source of the Spirit who animates the Church, which is built on the confession of faith by Peter. Here is the place where Peter offered his blood for the love of Jesus Christ and his brethren.

Let us pray
(silent pause)

You have called us to be part of the Church,
the presence of Christ in the world,
through our visit to the tomb of Peter,
help us to grow in faith, hope and charity,
under the guidance
of the Successor of the Prince of the Apostles.
Through Christ our Lord.
Amen.

The pilgrims, in procession, move towards the Holy Door while singing the Litany of the Saints (p. 227) or any other hymn.

The singing comes to an end before entering the Holy Door. In silence each pilgrim goes through the Holy Door.

Once the pilgrims have been through the Holy Door, they gather in front of the PIETÀ *to pray to the Mother of our Redeemer.*

O Holy Mother of our Redeemer,
heaven's gate, and star of the sea,
assist your people in their yearning for the resurrection.
Having accepted the greeting of the angel,
amidst the wonder of all creation,
you gave birth to your Creator,
Mother always virgin,
have pity on us sinners.

While a hymn is sung, the procession continues in the aisle of the Basilica.

Son of God, Light of the world,
Why do you sink before my eyes, O Lamb of God?
(Byzantine Liturgy for Holy Friday)
PIETÀ, Michelangelo, Saint Peter's, Rome

In the Basilica

Choose one of the following:

• *Celebration of the Mass (p. 45).*
• *Morning Prayer or Evening Prayer (p. 45).*
• *Liturgy of the Word (p. 40).*

Liturgy of the Word

Introduction

When the pilgrims are gathered in the Basilica, the celebration starts with the recitation of a psalm or the singing of a hymn. The animator says:

Let us turn our heart to Christ, who loves us and has washed away our sins with his blood. He made us a kingdom of priests to God our Father.

℟ To Him be glory and power
    For ever and ever. Amen.   (cf. Rev 1, 5–6)

Let us pray
(silent pause)

Grant us, O Lord,
that in the midst of the world's changes,
your Church, which you have founded on the rock,
through the profession of Peter,
will remain always steadfast.
Through Christ our Lord.

℟ Amen.

The Word of God

From the First Letter of Saint Peter

(2, 4–5.9–10)

He is the living stone, rejected by human beings but

chosen by God and precious to him; set yourselves
close to him so that you, too, may be living stones
making a spiritual house as a holy priesthood to offer
the spiritual sacrifices made acceptable to God through
Jesus Christ.

But you are a chosen race, a kingdom of priests, a
holy nation, a people to be a personal possession to
sing the praises of God who called you out of the darkness into his wonderful light. Once you were a non-
people now you are the People of God; once you were
outside his pity, now you have received his pity.

Canticle (cf. Col 1, 12–14.18–20)

℟ In Christ the Father has chosen us to be his sons.

We give thanks to the Father,
who has qualified us to share
in the inheritance of the saints in light.

℟ In Christ the Father has chosen us to be his sons.

He has delivered us from the dominion of darkness
and transferred us to the kingdom of his beloved Son,
in whom we have redemption, the forgiveness of sins.

℟ In Christ the Father has chosen us to be his sons.

He is the head of the body, the Church;
He is the beginning, the first-born from the dead,
that in everything he might be pre-eminent.

℟ In Christ the Father has chosen us to be his sons.

For in him all the fullness of God was pleased to dwell,
and through him to reconcile to himself all things,
whether on earth or in heaven, making peace by
    the blood of his cross.

℟ In Christ the Father has chosen us to be his sons.

A reading from the Gospel according to Matthew.

(16, 13–19)

Now when Jesus came into the district of Caesarea Philippi, he asked his disciples, "Who do men say that the Son of man is?" And they said, "Some say John the Baptist, others say Elijah, and others Jeremiah or one of the prophets". He said to them, "But who do you say that I am?" Simon Peter replied, "You are the Christ, the Son of the living God".

And Jesus answered him, "Blessed are you, Simon Bar-Jona! For flesh and blood has not revealed this to you, but my Father who is in heaven. And I tell you, you are Peter, and on this rock I will build my church, and the powers of death shall not prevail against it. I will give you the keys of the kingdom of heaven, and whatever you bind on earth shall be bound in heaven, and whatever you loose on earth shall be loosed in heaven".

The animator briefly traces out the meaning of the readings. A silent pause follows. If it is not possible to visit the tomb of Saint Peter after the Intercessions, *a hymn is sung or the* Credo *recited (p. 131).*

Intercessions

In the name of all those who are consecrated to God, let us pray to Him that each one may discover in the profession of the one true faith in Jesus Christ the courage to be a witness to the Gospel.

Lord, hear us: ℟ *Lord, graciously hear us.*

For the Church all over the world: may the grace of the Jubilee be an experience of growth in faith, hope and charity. Lord, hear us:

℟ *Lord, graciously hear us.*

For the Pope, the successor of the Apostle Peter, called to preside over the communion of all the Church: may the Lord strengthen him in his ministry. Lord, hear us:

℟ *Lord, graciously hear us.*

"Simon son of John, do you love me more than these others do?"
"Lord, you know everything; you know I love you" (Jn 21, 15.17)
Tapestry (Raphael's design), Vatican Museums, Rome

For the Bishops, the successors of the Apostles: may they be wise leaders to their Churches, zealously witnessing to the love of Christ, the good shepherd. Lord, hear us:

℟ *Lord, graciously hear us.*

For all the baptized, reborn to new life through water and the Holy Spirit: may they cooperate according to their call towards the building of the body of Christ. Lord, hear us:

℟ *Lord, graciously hear us.*

For all the pilgrims gathered in prayer in front of the tomb of the Apostle Peter: purified in the spirit, may they obtain grace to announce their faith through their life. Lord, hear us:

℟ *Lord, graciously hear us.*

And now let us join our praise and our petitions to God Almighty in the prayer that Jesus himself left to his Church:

Our Father.

O Lord, you have given to your Apostle Peter
the keys of the kingdom of heaven
and the power to bind and to loose,
grant us, through his intercession, victory over sin
and true freedom of the spirit.
Through Christ our Lord.

℟ *Amen.*

Profession of Faith

While approaching the tomb of Saint Peter, a psalm or a hymn is sung. With these, or similar, words the profession of faith is introduced:

Brothers and sisters, strengthened by the witness and the intercession of the Apostle Peter, let us profess our catholic faith:

Credo *(p. 131).*
At the end the hymn Tu es Petrus *is sung (p. 245).*

Celebration of the Mass

One of the following Masses, votive or for various occasions, can be celebrated if the liturgical norms allow it.

* For the Holy Year *(pp. 142–148)*.
From the Roman Missal:

* Apostle Saint Peter. *(p. 151)*.
* The Chair of Saint Peter.
* For the Church.
* For the Pope.
From the Masses of Our Lady:

* Our Lady, Queen of the Apostles.

If Mass is being said in the crypt, after the homily the Credo *can be sung, introduced with these, or similar, words:*

Brothers and sisters, strengthened by the witness and the intercession of the Apostle Peter, let us profess our catholic faith:

Credo *(p. 131)*.

If the Mass is said on one of the altars in the Basilica, at the end of the Mass, before the final benediction, the pilgrims, singing Tu es Petrus, *proceed to the altar of the* Confessio. *Here, the* Credo, *similarly introduced, can be sung. After the profession of faith, the celebrant gives the final blessing.*

During the Intercessions *a special prayer is said for the intention of the Pope.*

Morning and Evening Prayer

See p. 170. Instead of the short reading, use the reading on p. 40.

After the short homily, the Credo *is sung.*

There follows the Gospel Canticle *and then the* Intercessions, *among which a prayer for the intention of the Pope is included.*

After the singing of the Our Father, *the celebrant recites the final prayer (p. 44).*

IC̃.

SCS PAVLVS.

✠ IN NOMINE
TRVONE
CENVELE
CTRTVRCA
ELESTIVM
TENESTRIVET
INFERNORVM

UET
TCH
NEDI
ZIP
TRI
ME

SAINT PAUL
OUTSIDE THE WALLS

This celebration,
having as a theme
"the proclamation of Jesus Christ",
can take place,
with the necessary changes,
in a church within·the diocese
dedicated to Saint Paul
or to an apostle or a saint
distinguished in the
field of evangelization.

The divine mission which was given to me for you,
to make the word of God fully known,
which is Christ in you, the hope of glory
(Col 1, 25.27)
MAIN APSE, Saint Paul outside the Walls, Rome

ECESSITAS MIHI INCUMBIT

(1 Cor 9, 16)

The duty of announcing Christ

Reflection

"He moved from one place to another without stopping, pressing some, reaching out to others, faster than the wind. He governed as if the whole world were one ship, lifting those who are sinking, helping those who are falling, ordering the sailors. Sitting on the stern he kept watch on the bow, pulling the ropes. He manoeuvred the oars, stretched out the sails with his eyes on heaven, acting as boatswain, controlling the sails and the ship."

Thus, Saint John Chrysostom describes Saint Paul, the tireless evangelizer, making his way along the roads of the Roman Empire and the routes of the Mediterranean, firmly believing that his duty was to announce Christ (1 Cor 9, 16). Deeply united with his Jewish roots, after his conversion he brought with him this total dedication to Jesus: it is enough to recall that out of 535 uses of the word "Christ" in the New Testament, at least 400 are found in Saint Paul's letters.

Two autobiographical phrases capture the depth of his total dedication to Jesus: "I am alive; yet it is no longer I, but Christ living in me ... For me, to live is Christ" (Gal 2, 20; Phil 1, 21). Everything started with that voice on the road to Damascus: "Saul, Saul, why are you persecuting me?" (Acts 9, 4), an experience that the Apostle himself describes with three verbs, two indicating light, one expressing conflict: "Last of all he appeared to me... God chose to reveal his Son to me ... Christ Jesus took hold of me" (1 Cor 15, 8; Gal 1, 16; Phil 3, 12).

From that moment his life has been an all out struggle for the Gospel, as he himself confesses in his testament to Timothy: "My blood has been poured out as a libation, and the time has come for me to depart. I have fought the good fight to the end; I have run the race to the finish; I have kept the faith" (2 Tim 4, 6–7).

A life which had as its centre the death and resurrection of Jesus Christ, without which "our preaching is without substance, and so is your faith" (1 Cor 15, 14). A life full of human adventures, trials and sufferings, yet always under the guidance of that unerring star: "Can anything cut us off from the love of Christ - can hardships or distress, or persecution, or lack of food and clothing, or threats or violence? ... No; we come through all these things triumphantly victorious, by the power of him who loved us. For I am certain of this: neither death nor life, nor angels, nor principalities, nothing already in existence and nothing still to come, nor any power, nor the heights nor the depths, nor any created thing whatever, will be able to come between us and the love of God, known to us in Christ Jesus our Lord" (Rom 8, 35–39).

Paul's witness is still alive among us today through his letters, written, as he says, "not with ink but with the Spirit of the living God; not on stone tablets but on the tablets of human hearts" (2 Cor 3, 3).

His masterpiece, the Letter to the Romans, has been with the Church through the ages, especially the most difficult ones. Certain passages, especially his hymn to Christian love in chapter 13 of the First Letter to the Corinthians, illuminate the path of faith and sustain the hope of Christianity.

The seal of his martyrdom in Rome is glimpsed in some of his letters. Like the note he writes to Philemon, where he describes himself as "an old man, and now also a prisoner of Christ Jesus" (v. 9). On his tombstone we can inscribe two epigraphs. The first is the summary of his life: "God, who chose me in my mother's womb, called me through his grace and chose to reveal his Son to me, so that I should preach him to the gentiles" (Gal 1, 15–16). The second is the summary of his faith: "Jesus Christ, the same yesterday, today and for ever" (Heb 13, 8).

Go, therefore, make disciples of all nations (Mt 28, 19)
A wooden statue, the lower part of which
pilgrims have bitten off
WOODEN STATUE OF SAINT PAUL, Saint Paul outside the Walls, Rome

ON POSSUMUS NON LOQUI (Acts 4, 20)

We cannot remain silent

Celebration

Towards the Basilica

The pilgrims will gather outside the church. The animator leads the prayer with Psalm 67:

℟ Let the peoples praise you, O God;
let all the peoples praise you.

O God, be gracious and bless us
and let your face shed its light upon us.
So will your ways be known upon earth
and all nations learn your saving help. ℟

Let the nations be glad and exult
for you rule the world with justice.
With fairness you rule the peoples,
you guide the nations on earth. ℟

The earth has yielded its fruit,
for God, our God, has blessed us.
May God still give us his blessing
till the ends of the earth revere him. ℟

Glory. ℟

The animator recalls the meaning of going through the Holy Door and the visit to the Basilica of Saint Paul with these, or similar, words:

With gratitude to God our Father for the gift of the Gospel handed down to us by the Apostles, "we cannot stop proclaiming" (Acts 4, 20) that which we have heard in faith. Visiting the places recalling the Roman experience of Saint Paul, we would like to ask for the grace of being evangelizers taking on ourselves the mission to proclaim Jesus Christ to those who have not yet heard of him.

Let us pray
(silent pause)

God our Father,
you have sent Christ,
true light, into the world,
may your Holy Spirit increase
the desire for truth in the hearts of all
and encourage obedience founded on faith,
so that all who have been reborn in Baptism
may form the one and everlasting covenant.
Through Christ our Lord.
℞ Amen.

The pilgrims, in procession, move towards the Holy Door while singing the Litany of the Saints *(p. 227) or the* Invocations to Jesus our Saviour *(p. 224) or any other hymn.*

The singing comes to an end before entering the Holy Door. In silence each pilgrim goes through the Holy Door.

Once the pilgrims have been through the Holy Door, singing resumes and the pilgrims proceed to the altar of Confession where the following prayer is said:

Lord God, Almighty Father,
who chose the Apostle Paul
to spread the good news,
may all people be enlightened by the faith
that he proclaimed
to kings and nations,
and may your Church be always
a mother and teacher to all nations.
Through Christ our Lord.
℞ Amen.

The animator recalls the spiritual meaning of the Basilica in relation to the Jubilee Year.

In the Basilica

Choose one of the following:
- *Celebration of the Mass (p. 59).*
- *Morning Prayer or Evening Prayer (p. 59).*
- *Liturgy of the Word (p.53).*

Liturgy of the Word

Introduction

When the pilgrims are gathered in the Basilica, the celebration starts with the recitation of a psalm or the singing of a hymn. The animator says:

At the name of Jesus every knee shall bow
in heaven, on earth and under the earth.

℟ And every tongue confess that Jesus is Lord,
to the glory of God the Father. (cf. Phil 2, 6–11)

Let us pray
(silent pause)

O Lord, you have founded the Church
as a universal sacrament of salvation
to continue to the end of time
what Christ has done,
awaken the hearts of your faithful
to become missionaries
so that from all the peoples of the world
one family, a new humanity, is formed
in Christ our Lord.
Who lives and reigns for ever and ever.

℟ Amen.

The Word of God

From the Letter of Saint Paul to the Colossians

(1, 24–28)

It makes me happy to be suffering for you now, and in my own body to make up all the hardships that still have to be undergone by Christ for the sake of his body, the Church, of which I was made a servant with the responsibility towards you that God gave to me, that of completing God's message, the message which was a mystery hidden for generations and centuries and has now been revealed to his holy people.

It was God's purpose to reveal to them how rich is the glory of this mystery among the Gentiles; it is Christ among you, your hope of glory: this is the Christ we are proclaiming, admonishing and instructing everyone in all wisdom, to make everyone perfect in Christ.

Canticle   (cf. Rev 15, 3–4)

℟ Your salvation, O Lord, is for all the nations.

Great and wonderful are all your works,
Lord God Almighty;
upright and true are all your ways,
    King of nations.   ℟

Who does not revere
and glorify your name, O Lord?
For you alone are holy.   ℟

All nations will come and adore you
for the many acts
of saving justice you have shown.   ℟

In my own body I make up all the hardships that still have to be undergone by Christ for the sake of his body, the Church (Col 1, 24)
WOODEN CRUCIFIX, Saint Paul outside the Walls, Rome

A reading from the Gospel according to Matthew

(28, 16–20)

Meanwhile the eleven disciples set out for Galilee, to the mountain where Jesus had arranged to meet them. When they saw him they fell down before him, though some hesitated. Jesus came up and spoke to them. He said: "All authority in heaven and on earth has been given to me. Go, therefore, make disciples of all nations; baptize them in the name of the Father and of the Son and of the Holy Spirit, and teach them to observe all the commands I gave you. And look, I am with you always; yes, to the end of time."

The animator briefly traces out the meaning of the readings. A silent pause follows. If it is not possible to visit the tomb of the Apostle, after the Intercessions, *a hymn is sung or the* Credo *is recited (p. 131).*

Intercessions

Animated by the Spirit who guides our prayer, let us ask our heavenly Father that the light of the Gospel of Jesus Christ may reach the whole earth.
Lord, hear us:

℟ *Lord, graciously hear us.*

For all the baptized, that the grace of this Holy Year may renew their commitment in witness through word and deed that Christ is Lord. Lord, hear us:

℟ *Lord, graciously hear us.*

For the Pope, the Bishops, priests and ministers of the Good News, that their life may become a witness to their brethren. Lord, hear us:

℟ *Lord, graciously hear us.*

For young people, that they may generously accept the call to be missionaries of the word and proclaim it with enthusiasm to the world. Lord, hear us:

℟ *Lord, graciously hear us.*

Saul went to the high priest for authorization to arrest and take to Jerusalem any followers of the Way. He was led blind into Damascus, to Ananias, who gave him back his sight and baptized him. The Jews were keeping watch at the gates day and night in order to kill him, but the disciples let him down from the wall in a basket (cf. Acts 9, 1–25)

BIBLE OF CHARLES THE BALD, Monastery of Saint Paul, Rome

And now let us together ask God our Father that his
kingdom may come:

Our Father.

Almighty and eternal God,
may all those who do not know Jesus Christ,
through sincerity of heart,
arrive at the truth,
and grant us that we may grow into a deeper
    knowledge
of your mystery of salvation,
living it in charity among ourselves,
and so giving the world a credible witness of your
    love.
Through Christ our Lord.
℟ Amen.

Profession of Faith

While approaching the altar of the Confessio, *a psalm
or a hymn is sung. With these, or similar, words the
profession of faith is introduced:*

Brothers and sisters, remembering the anointing of
the Holy Spirit which has consecrated us as
witnesses of the Gospel, in communion with all
believers in Christ across the world, let us profess
our catholic faith:

Credo *(p. 131).*

The animator invites the pilgrims to pray:

And now let us ask the Virgin Mary, "star of evangelization":

Hail, Mary *(or a similar prayer, pp. 235-236).*

Celebration of the Mass

One of the following Masses, votive or for various occasions, can be celebrated if the liturgical norms allow it.

* For the Holy Year *(pp. 142-148)*.

From the Roman Missal:

* Apostle, Saint Paul *(p. 154)*.
* For the Spread of the Gospel.
* For the Church.
* For the Pope.

From the Masses of Our Lady:

* Visitation of Our Lady.
* Our Lady, Queen of the Apostles.

After the homily the Credo *can be recited, introduced with these, or similar, words:*

Brothers and sisters, remembering the anointing of the Holy Spirit which has consecrated us as witnesses of the Gospel, in communion with all believers in Christ across the world, let us profess our catholic faith:

Credo *(p. 131)*.

Or, at the end of the Mass, before the final benediction, the pilgrims gather in front of the altar of the Confessio. *Here, the* Credo, *similarly introduced, can be sung, followed by a Marian prayer (pp. 235–236). Then the celebrant gives the final blessing.*

During the Intercessions *a special prayer is said for the intention of the Pope.*

Morning and Evening Prayer

See p. 170. Instead of the short reading, use the reading on p. 54.

After the short homily, the Credo *is sung.*

There follows the Gospel Canticle *and then the* Intercessions, *among which a prayer for the intention of the Pope is included.*

After the singing of the Our Father, *the celebrant recites the final prayer (p. 58).*

SAINT JOHN LATERAN

This celebration,
having as a theme
"one body in Christ",
can take place,
adapted as necessary,
in a church within the diocese
dedicated to Saint John or to
a saint who worked
for church unity and
communion.

In truth I tell you, of all the children born to
women, there has never been anyone greater
than John the Baptist (Mt 11, 11)
Main Apse, Saint John Lateran, Rome

EUS CARITAS EST (1 Jn 4, 8)

God is love

Reflection

"We therefore make bold to say that the Gospels are the flower of the Scriptures, and among the Gospels that of John is the flower. No one can reach the depth of the meaning of it except he has lain on Jesus' breast." Thus the great Origen of Alexandria described the fourth Gospel, to which tradition gives the symbol of the eagle for its elevated thoughts on the mystery of the Word of God: "In the beginning was the Word: the Word was with God and the Word was God" (Jn 1, 1).

These pages, that the Greek original presents in 15,416 words, reflect the face of John, the "beloved disciple" of Jesus, who on Calvary, following the last words of Jesus, accepted Mary as his mother. It is on him and his writings that we reflect even though the church is dedicated also to the Divine Saviour and Saint John the Baptist.

The fourth Gospel, with its complex history, in a way expresses the faith of the churches in Asia Minor. With it we also have the three letters of John and the Book of Revelation, also known as the Apocalypse.

Within these writings there are many events, themes, symbols and messages. From them we choose one to represent John. It may serve as an invitation for all to follow since it takes the form of a motto. It is the new "commandment" which Christ left as a last message to his disciples while he was with them on that last evening of his human story: "This is my commandment: love one another, as I have loved you" (15, 12). The rule of Christian love goes well beyond that of the Old Testament: "You shall love your neighbour as yourself" (Mt 19, 19). It is a rule which is complete and full of paradox: "This is my commandment: love one another, as I have loved you. No one can have greater love than to lay down his life for his friends" (Jn 15, 12–13). Jesus' last words on that evening are a hymn to a love which is able to embrace time and enlighten the historical backdrop against which Christians have to live their call. And Christ is already aware of the challenge and the danger of division: "May they all be one, just as, Father, you are in me and I am in you, so that they also may be in us ..." (Jn 17, 21).

This prayer, which for us and for all the Christian Churches sounds as an appeal to search constantly for unity and love, is frequent in Saint John's letters.

It seems that the Apostle is repeating only one word to his "children", that is to the young generations of believers and also to us: "God is love" (1 Jn 4, 8), therefore "We must love one another ... This is the proof of love, that he laid down his life for us, and we too ought to lay down our lives for our brothers ... Let us love, then, because he first loved us. Anyone who says 'I love God' and hates his brother is a liar, since whoever does not love the brother whom he can see cannot love God whom he has not seen. Indeed this is the commandment we have received from him, that whoever loves God, must also love his brother" (1 Jn 3, 11.16; 4, 19–21).

Faith and love necessarily recall each other. On this conviction Saint John launches his message to the Church that in unity all Christians may strive to be one in faith and united in love: "His commandment is this, that we should believe in the name of his Son Jesus Christ and that we should love one another as he commanded us" (1 Jn 3, 23).

*John to the Churches: grace and peace to you from him who is,
who was, and who is to come, and from Jesus Christ,
the first-born from the dead* (Rev 1, 4–5)

SAINT JOHN THE EVANGELIST, G. B. Della Porta,
Saint John Lateran, Rome

NUM CORPUS (Eph 4, 4)

One Body in Christ

Celebration

Towards the Basilica

The pilgrims are gathered outside the church. The animator leads the prayer with Psalm 95:

℟ Come, ring out our joy to the Lord,
   let us listen to his voice.

Come, ring out our joy to the Lord;
hail the rock who saves us.
Let us come before him, giving thanks,
with songs let us hail the Lord. ℟

A mighty God is the Lord,
a great king above all gods.
In his hands are the depths of the earth;
the heights of the mountains are his.
To him belongs the sea, for he made it,
and the dry land shaped by his hands. ℟

Come in; let us bow and bend low;
let us kneel before the God who made us;
for he is our God and we
the people who belong to his pasture,
the flock that is led by his hand. ℟

O that today you would listen to his voice!
"Harden not your hearts as at Meribah,
as on that day at Massah in the desert
when your fathers put me to the test;
when they tried me, though they saw my work." ℟

Glory. ℟

The animator with these, or similar, words recalls the meaning of going through the Holy Door and the visit to the Cathedral of Rome, Mother Church of all the Churches:

The sacrament of Baptism is the foundation on which the communion between all Christians is founded, even among those who are not in full communion with the Catholic Church. Aware of the grace of Baptism, which has made us one with Christ, like branches to the one vine, let us prepare ourselves to go through the Holy Door with an attitude of thanksgiving and of forgiveness: we thank God for the gift of faith; we ask forgiveness for the divisions between us Christians.

Let us pray
(silent pause)

Lord, Creator and Father,
you unite the dispersed and guard them in unity,
look favourably on the flock of your Son,
so that all who are consecrated in the one Baptism
will be one family
in the unity of love and true faith.
Through Christ our Lord.

℟ Amen.

The pilgrims, in procession, move towards the Holy Door while singing the Litany of the Saints *(p. 227) or the* Invocations to Christ the Saviour *(p. 224) or any other hymn.*

The singing comes to an end before arrival at the Holy Door. In silence each pilgrim goes through the Holy Door.

Once the pilgrims have been through the Holy Door, singing resumes and they proceed to the main altar where the following prayer is said:

Lord Jesus, you wanted to call your Church
the multitude of believers,
may those who are gathered here in your name
adore you, love you, follow you,
so that under your guiding hand
they may reach what you promise.
To you who live and reign with the Father and the
    Holy Spirit
all honour and glory for ever and ever.

℟ Amen

The animator recalls the spiritual meaning of the Basilica in relation to the Jubilee Year.

In the Basilica

Choose one of the following:

- *Celebration of the Mass (p. 73).*
- *Morning Prayer or Evening Prayer (p. 73).*
- *Liturgy of the Word (p. 67).*

Liturgy of the Word

Introduction

When the pilgrims are gathered in the Basilica, the celebration starts with the recitation of a psalm or the singing of a hymn. The animator says:

Let us give praise to God, whose power is far greater than what we can ask or think, that His Spirit may be at work in us.

℟ Glory be to him in the Church and in Christ Jesus for ever and ever. Amen.   (cf. Eph 3, 20–21)

Let us pray
(silent pause)

Pour out upon us, O Father,
the glory of your love,
and by the power of your Spirit
end the divisions between Christians,
that your Church may be seen
as a sign lifted up among the peoples,
and the human race, enlightened by your Spirit,
may believe in the God who sent
Jesus Christ, your Son, our Saviour.
Who lives and reigns with you,
in the unity of the Holy Spirit,
for ever and ever.

℟ Amen.

The Word of God

From the Letter of Saint Paul to the Ephesians (4, 1–6)

I, the prisoner in the Lord, urge you therefore to lead a life worthy of the vocation to which you were called. With all humility and gentleness, and with patience, support each other in love. Take every care to preserve the unity of the Spirit by the peace that binds you together. There is one Body, one Spirit, just as one hope is the goal of your calling by God. There is one Lord, one faith, one baptism, and one God and Father of all, over all, through all and within all.

Psalm 122

℟ Strengthen, O Lord, the unity of your people.

I rejoiced when I heard them say:
"Let us go to God's house."
And now our feet are standing
within your gates, O Jerusalem. ℟

Jerusalem is built as a city
strongly compact.
It is there that the tribes go up,
the tribes of the Lord. ℟

For Israel's law it is,
there to praise the Lord's name.
There were set the thrones of judgment
of the house of David. ℟

For the peace of Jerusalem pray:
"Peace be to your homes!
May peace reign within your walls,
in your palaces, peace!" ℟

For love of my brethren and friends
I say: "Peace upon you."
For love of the house of the Lord
I will ask for your good. ℟

A reading from the Gospel according to John
(17,1.20–23)

Jesus raised his eyes to heaven and said:

"Father, I pray not only for these but also for those who through their teaching will come to believe in me. May they all be one, just as, Father, you are in me and I am in you, so that they also may be in us, so that the world may believe it was you who sent me.

"I have given them the glory you gave to me, that they may be one as we are one. With me in them and you in me, may they be so perfected in unity that the world will recognize that it was you who sent me and that you have loved them as you have loved me."

The animator briefly traces out the meaning of the readings. A silent pause follows.

Profession of Faith

The Credo *is sung (p. 131) or, instead, the Renewal of* Baptismal Vows is made.

Brothers and sisters, mindful of being one with Christ, let the renewal of our baptismal promises strengthen our faithful commitment to God as we live it in the Church.

Priest: Do you reject Satan?

All: I do.

Priest: And all his works?

All: I do.

Priest: And all his empty promises?

All: I do.

Priest: Do you believe in God, the Father almighty, Creator of heaven and earth?

All: I do.

Priest: Do you believe in Jesus Christ,
his only Son, our Lord,
who was born of the Virgin Mary,
was crucified, died, and was buried,
rose from the dead.
and is now seated at the right hand of the Father?

All: I do.

Priest: Do you believe in the Holy Spirit,
the holy catholic Church, the communion of saints,
the forgiveness of sins, the resurrection of the body,
and life everlasting?

All: I do.

At the end the Priest says:

This is our faith. This is the faith of the Church. We are
proud to profess it, in Christ Jesus our Lord. ℟ Amen.

*Then the Priest blesses the pilgrims with holy water while a
hymn is sung by the assembly.*

Intercessions

Let us pray to God for all the believers in Christ, that
the presence of him who has died for our sins may be
a source of encouragement towards the communion
of faith and love. Lord, hear us:

℟ *Lord, graciously hear us.*

For all Christians, that through obedience to the word
of Jesus they may strive to enrich the gift of unity. Lord,
hear us. ℟

For the Pope, that under the guidance of the Holy Spirit
he may fulfil the mission entrusted to him by Christ
who has chosen him as the successor of Peter. Lord,
hear us. ℟

For the Bishops, that they may be promoters of unity
between all believers in Jesus Christ. Lord, hear us. ℟

For our brethren belonging to the Orthodox Churches
of the East, that the sharing of the one Baptism will

leave its mark of love on the hearts for the benefit of the unity of the Church. Lord, hear us. ℟.

For our brethren of the West who are not in full communion with the Catholic Church, that faithfulness to the Gospel will inspire new ways of fraternal communion. Lord, hear us. ℟.

For all those who do know Christ, that the desire to grow in unity will be to them a stronger witness than the scandal of division within the Churches. Lord, hear us. ℟.

For all those who are suffering because of the Gospel, that in their time of trial they will find support and sustenance in the common intercession of faith from their brothers and sisters. Lord, hear us. ℟.

For us and all the pilgrims who visit this Basilica for a moment of prayer, that drawing from the source of the Spirit we may grow in the love of our neighbour. Lord, hear us. ℟.

And now let us present all our petitions to our common Father:

Our Father.

Hear, O Lord, our prayer
and unite the hearts of all your faithful.
While they honour your name
and commit themselves to conversion,
assist them so that every division may be overcome,
that your Church, forming again a perfect communion,
may, in the joy of Christ, go forward towards
　　your kingdom.
Who lives and reigns for ever and ever.　　℟. Amen.

The animator invites the pilgrims to remember the Mother of the Lord:

And now let us turn our thoughts
to the Mother of the Lord, first fruit of the Church,
that she may guide all believers towards unity:

Hail, Mary *(or any other invocation, pp. 235–236).*

*I am the disciple of a Holy Shepherd who has wide eyes,
and his glance reaches everywhere* (Inscription of Abercius)
FACE OF JESUS "not painted by human hands",
Saint John Lateran, Rome

Celebration of the Mass

One of the following Masses, votive or for various occasions, can be celebrated if the liturgical norms allow it.

* For the Holy Year *(pp. 142–148).*

From the Roman Missal:
* The Universal Church *(p. 155).*
* For Unity of Christians *(3 formularies).*
* For the Pope.

From the Masses of Our Lady:
* The Virgin Mary, Mother of Unity.

After the homily, there can be the singing of the Credo *(p. 131) or – except during Lent – the* Renewal of Baptismal Vows *(p. 69).*

Or, at the end of the Mass, before the final benediction, the pilgrims gather in the central nave of the Church where the Credo *is sung, followed by a Marian prayer (pp. 235–236). After the profession of faith, the celebrant gives the final blessing.*

During the Intercessions *a special prayer is said for the intention of the Pope.*

Morning and Evening Prayer

See p. 170. Instead of the short reading, use the reading shown on p. 68.

After the homily, there can be the singing of the Credo *or the* Renewal of Baptismal Vows. *There follows the* Gospel Canticle *and then the* Intercessions, *among which a prayer for the intention of the Pope is included.*

After the singing of the Our Father, *the celebrant recites the final prayer (p. 71).*

SANTA MARIA MAGGIORE

*This celebration,
having as its theme
"meeting Christ with Mary",
can take place, adapted as
necessary, in a Marian shrine
of the diocese or in a church
dedicated to the Virgin Mary.*

*Hail, O Star which brings forth the sun
Hail, O Womb where God is made man
Hail, O Mother of the eternal Star
Hail, O rising sun of the mysterious Day*
(Romanos Melodos, *Akathistos Hymn*)
BIRTH OF JESUS, I. Torriti,
Santa Maria Maggiore, Rome

ARIA ABIIT IN MONTANA (Lk 1, 39)

On pilgrimage with Mary

Reflection

"I would like your icon, O Mother of God, to be continually reflected in the mirror of the heart and to treasure it until the end of time. Raise those who are down-hearted and give hope to those who contemplate the eternal beauty." This is a prayer of a Greek mystic of the fifth century called Pseudo-Dionysius the Areopagite.

Mary's icon is represented in thousands of faces in the history and tradition of Christian devotion. Here is one aspect which is particularly insisted on in the Gospels: the Mother of the Lord is frequently presented as a pilgrim. Hers is a pilgrimage in faith which takes place in time (cf. *Redemptoris Mater* 25).

Right from her very first appearance in the Gospels she is on a pilgrimage: on her way to a town in Judah where her cousin Elizabeth lives (cf. Lk 1, 39). She is also on a pilgrimage immediately after, with Joseph her husband, towards Bethlehem for the census, but also to deliver to the world and to history Christ the Saviour. And again, after a few days, she is on a pilgrimage with her poor family towards Egypt, living the experience of so many refugees, persecuted people and immigrants through the ages.

On her return to Nazareth, Mary, together with so many Jews, is on another pilgrimage, this time to the temple of Jerusalem: here the mystery of the Son is made manifest, that Son to whom she gave birth but who does not belong to her. And when Christ begins his mission announcing the good news of salvation to the poor and the year of favour from God, that is the perfect Jubilee of freedom from sin, Mary is the silent pilgrim following Jesus' steps. She rarely appears in the Gospels. She is present in Cana during the wedding, where the first glorious "sign" takes place, but it is a rather timid presence.

On another occasion, it is an anonymous woman who signals to those present and to Jesus that Mary is there – amongst the crowd: "Blessed the womb that bore you and the breasts that fed you!" (Lk 11, 27).

And Jesus outlines the perfect profile of the Mother, a model to all those who decide to walk the journey of faith: "More blessed still are those who hear the word of God and keep it!" (Lk 11, 28). It is a beatitude that echoes the greeting of Elizabeth: "Blessed is she who believed that the promise made her by the Lord would be fulfilled" (Lk 1, 45). Mary's pilgrimage reaches the most difficult destination on a Friday afternoon on a hill called Golgotha. There, the last visible encounter between the Mother and her Son takes place.

At the very moment when Mary loses Him whom she had borne (her life was a gradual and continuous letting go of the "possession" of her Son), she receives another son, rather all the sons and daughters of the Church: "Woman, this is your son ... This is your mother" (Jn 19, 26–27).

From that moment, "that face, so charming and bright, of which it is so difficult to resist the beauty", as described by Pseudo-Matthew (fourth–fifth century), is a reminder to believers in Christ: like her and with her all Christians are pilgrims on the journey of faith, with the hope of meeting her one day.

An eighth-century Muslim mystic from Iraq, Rabi'a, said: "On the day of judgment, at the head of all there will be Mary the believer: may there be peace on her and on all those who believe!"

*She gave birth to a son, her first-born, she wrapped him
in swaddling clothes and laid him in a manger* (Lk 2, 7)
RELIQUARY OF THE MANGER OF BETHLEHEM,
Santa Maria Maggiore, Rome

**CCEPIT EAM DISCIPULUS IN SUA** (Jn 19, 27)

Welcoming Mary

Celebration

Towards the Basilica

The pilgrims are gathered outside the church. The animator leads the prayer with Psalm 116:

℟. Come let us adore Christ the Lord,
   Son of the Virgin Mary.

How can I repay the Lord
for his goodness to me?
The cup of salvation I will raise;
I will call on the Lord's name. ℟.

Your servant, Lord, your servant am I;
you have loosened my bonds.
A thanksgiving sacrifice I make;
I will call on the Lord's name. ℟.

My vows to the Lord I will fulfil
before all his people,
in the courts of the house of the Lord,
in your midst, O Jerusalem. ℟.

Glory. ℟.

The animator with these, or similar, words recalls the meaning of going through the Holy Door and the visit to the Basilica:

While thanking God for the gift of His Son, we will not fail to thank Mary. Through her "yes" to the angel, through the Holy Spirit she became the Mother of God and in that night in Bethlehem "the eternal light shone to the world, Jesus Christ our Saviour". As we visit the oldest Marian shrine in the West, let us ask Mary's help so that our hearts will always be the temple of the Most High.

Let us pray
(silent pause)

O God Almighty,
who in the womb of the Virgin Mary
has prepared a shrine for Christ your Son,
help us to keep alive the grace of Baptism
so that we adore you in spirit and in truth
and become a temple of your glory.
Through Christ our Lord.

℟. Amen

*The pilgrims, in procession, move towards the Holy Door
while singing the* Litany to the Blessed Virgin Mary *(p. 231)
or another hymn.*

*The singing comes to an end before arrival at the Holy Door.
In silence each pilgrim goes through the Holy Door.*

*Once the pilgrims have been through the Holy Door, singing
resumes and the procession continues towards the icon of
Our Lady "Salus populi romani".*

We turn to you for protection,
holy Mother of God.
Listen to our prayers
and help us in our needs.
Save us from every danger,
glorious and blessed Virgin.

*The animator recalls the spiritual meaning of the Basilica
in relation to the Jubilee Year.*

*Hail, you gave yourself as a throne to the king.
Hail, you hold the one who holds the world.*
(Romanos Melodos, *Akathistos Hymn*)
SALUS POPULI ROMANI, Santa Maria Maggiore, Rome

In the Basilica

Choose one of the following:
- *Celebration of the Mass (p. 87).*
- *Morning Prayer or Evening Prayer (p. 87).*
- *Liturgy of the Word (p. 82).*

Liturgy of the Word

Introduction

When the pilgrims are gathered in the Basilica, the celebration starts with the recitation of the Angelus *(p. 233).*

The Word of God

From the Letter of Saint Paul to the Galatians (4,4–7)

Brothers, when the completion of the time came, God sent his Son, born of a woman, born a subject of the Law, to redeem the subjects of the Law, so that we could receive adoption as sons. As you are sons, God has sent into our hearts the Spirit of his Son crying, "Abba, Father"; and so you are no longer a slave, but a son; and if a son, then an heir, by God's own act.

Psalm 22

℟ From my mother's womb you have been my God.

In you our fathers put their trust;
they trusted and you set them free.
When they cried to you, they escaped.
In you they trusted and never in vain. ℟
Yes, it was you who took me from the womb,
entrusted me to my mother's breast.

To you I was committed from my birth,
from my mother's womb you have been my God. ℟

I will tell of your name to my brethren
and praise you where they are assembled.
"You who fear the Lord give him praise;
all sons of Jacob, give him glory.
Revere him, Israel's sons." ℟

A reading from the Gospel according to Luke (2, 4–11)

So Joseph set out from the town of Nazareth in Galilee for Judaea, to David's town called Bethlehem, since he was of David's House and line, in order to be registered together with Mary, his betrothed, who was with child.

Now it happened that, while they were there, the time came for her to have her child, and she gave birth to a son, her first-born. She wrapped him in swaddling clothes and laid him in a manger because there was no room for them in the inn. In the countryside close by there were shepherds out in the fields keeping guard over their sheep during the watches of the night. An angel of the Lord stood over them and the glory of the Lord shone round them. They were terrified, but the angel said, "Do not be afraid. Look, I bring you news of great joy, a joy to be shared by the whole people. Today in the town of David a Saviour has been born to you; he is Christ the Lord."

The animator briefly traces out the meaning of the readings. A silent pause follows.

Profession of Faith

The whole group can sing the Magnificat *(p. 172) in front of the altar, after which the* Credo *can be introduced with the following words:*

Brothers and sisters, in communion with Mary, the first among the believers, let us profess our faith:

Credo *(p. 131).*

Hail, Essence of the King of the universe
Hail, O Lady who fills us with joy
(Joseph the Hymnographer, *Canon to the Akathistos Hymn*)
Main Apse, Santa Maria Maggiore, Rome

Intercessions

Facing the main apse, the animator introduces the following prayers:

Let us call upon Christ, the Lord of the universe, while seeking the intercession of his Mother, raised with him to the glory of heaven. Lord, hear us:

℟ May your holy Mother intercede for us.

Save us, Lord, by your incarnation. ℟

Save us, Lord, by your birth at Bethlehem. ℟

Save us, Lord, by your presentation at the temple. ℟

Save us, Lord, by your holy baptism. ℟

Save us, Lord, by your passion and cross. ℟

Save us, Lord, by your death and burial. ℟

Save us, Lord, by your holy resurrection. ℟

Save us, Lord, by your glorious ascension. ℟

Save us, Lord, for the gift of the Holy Spirit. ℟

Save us, Lord, when you come in glory. ℟

Grant to our Pope life and strength and preserve him to be for your holy Church a guide and a pastor for the people of God.

℟ May your holy Mother intercede for him.

Enlighten the minds of those who govern in the search for the common good, peace and justice.

℟ May your holy Mother intercede for them.

Listen to the suffering of the abandoned, the cry of those who are persecuted and the prayer of the innocent victims.

℟ May your holy Mother intercede for them.

Lead to conversion those who are away from you
through a fault of their own or because of the scan-
dals of others.

℟ May your holy Mother intercede for them.

Show the light of your face to all those who search for
you with a sincere heart.

℟ May your holy Mother intercede for them.

Our Father.

O God, you have revealed to the world your Son,
as the glory of Israel and light to the world,
in the arms of the Virgin Mother;
may we learn from her to strengthen our faith in Christ
and to recognize in Him the only mediator
and saviour of all humanity.
Who lives and reigns for ever and ever.

℟ Amen.

As a conclusion:

Act of Consecration to the Mother of the Lord

Obedient to the word of Jesus dying on the cross,
we give ourselves to you as sons and daughters,
O Mother of the Lord:
keep us close to you with your maternal love,
teach us the wisdom of the Gospel,
guide us to be united with Christ.

Celebration of the Mass

One of the following Masses, votive or for various occasions, can be celebrated if the liturgical norms allow it.

* For the Holy Year *(pp. 142-148).*

From the Roman Missal:

* Mary, Mother of God *(p. 149).*
* The Universal Church.
* For the Pope.

From the Masses of Our Lady:

* The Virgin Mary, Mother of the Redeemer.
* The Virgin Mary, New Woman.
* The Virgin Mary, Temple of the Lord.

After the homily, the Credo *can be sung (p. 131), introduced with these, or similar, words:*

Brothers and Sisters, in communion with Mary, first among believers, let us profess our faith: Credo

Or, at the end of the Mass, before the final benediction, the pilgrims gather in front of the main altar, where the Credo *is sung, followed by the* Act of Consecration to the Mother of the Lord. *Afterwards, the celebrant gives the final blessing.*

During the Intercessions *a special prayer is said for the intention of the Pope.*

Morning and Evening Prayer

See p. 170. Instead of the short reading, refer to the reading shown on p. 82. After a short homily there is the singing of the Credo; *there follows the* Gospel Canticle *and then the* Intercessions, *among which a prayer for the intention of the Pope is included. After the singing of the* Our Father, *the celebrant recites the following prayer:*

O God, through the fruitful virginity of Mary you have given to humanity the wealth of eternal salvation, may we experience the richness of her intercession, since it was through her that we have received the author of life, Christ your Son, who lives and reigns with you and the Holy Spirit, for ever and ever.

℟ Amen.

There follows the Act of Consecration to the Mother of the Lord (p. 86).

SANTA CROCE
IN GERUSALEMME

SAN LORENZO

*This celebration,
having as a theme*
"the Wisdom of the Cross of Christ",
*can take place, with the necessary
changes, in a church where
there is devotion to the
Cross, especially during
penitential days.*

Hail, O Cross, our only hope!
(Venantius Fortunatus, *Vexilla Regis*)
MAIN APSE, Antoniazzo Romano,
Santa Croce in Gerusalemme, Rome

XALTATUS A TERRA, OMNES TRAHAM AD ME IPSUM (Jn 12, 32)

When I am lifted up from the earth, I shall draw all people to myself

Reflection

"Although it is fixed on earth in one particular point, the cross of Christ spreads its rays in all directions."

These words of Gregory of Nyssa, fourth-century Father of the Church from Cappadocia (in today's Turkey), convey the strength of the suffering of Christ within the experience of evil and suffering in the world. There is a reflection of the words of Jesus: "When I am lifted up from the earth, I shall draw all people to myself" (Jn 12, 32).

Golgotha, the Place of the Skull, so called because of its shape, or because it is near a burial place, is a place in space and time where the Cross points towards heaven with its arms wide open reaching to the horizon. Another Christian writer of the early Church, Hippolytus of Rome (second century), in his Easter Homilies, points out how there is unity and redemption in the Cross: "The tree of the Cross from the earth grows towards heaven; it is the support of all things, the point of reference for the universe, that which unites the world."

Jesus in the night he met Nicodemus had already shown how strong is this force and how great is the freedom coming out of His Cross: "as Moses lifted up the snake in the desert, so must the Son of man be lifted up so that everyone who believes may have eternal life in him. For this is how God loved the world: he gave his only Son, so that everyone who believes in him may not perish but may have eternal life" (Jn 3, 14–16).

The moment Jesus entered the experience of suffering and death, these realities, typically "human", were given a new energy, were transformed. In them there is to be found, now, the seed of eternity and of salvation. That participation of Jesus has not diminished his glory; it has rather transfigured our limits and redeemed the dark side of our existence. For this reason Paul is not afraid of dying and considers it to be "gain" since "life to me, of course, is Christ" (Phil 1, 21). In this perspective the good news of the Gospel is centred on the tragic and glorious Cross of Jesus: "While the Jews demand miracles and the Greeks look for wisdom, we preach Christ crucified: to the Jews an obstacle they cannot get over, to the Gentiles foolishness, but to those who have been called, whether they are Jews or Greeks, a Christ who is both the power of God and the wisdom of God" (1 Cor 1, 22–24).

The way of the Cross is the pilgrimage of all Christians, remembering the words of Jesus: "If anyone wants to be a follower of mine, let him renounce himself and take up his cross and follow me" (Mt 16, 24).

The suffering and death that are on our horizon are not sterile and dismal experiences, because: "unless a wheat grain falls into the earth and dies, it remains only a single grain; but if it dies it yields a rich harvest" (Jn 12, 24). On the way of the Cross which draws every single person, there are also those who do not believe but yet continue to hope and search. Jorge L. Borges, an Argentinian writer, in his poem "Christ on the Cross" writes: "His face is not that of the painters. It is a hard face, a Jewish one. I do not see him but continue to look for him until the day of my last steps on earth."

All of us then, following the words of the Letter to the Hebrews, "let us go to him, then, outside the camp, and bear his humiliation" of the Cross (13, 13). It is towards that wood that the martyrs turned their hope: "May the People of God, confirmed in faith by the example of these true champions of every age, language and nation, cross with full confidence the threshold of the Third Millennium" (IM 13).

Towards Golgotha (on Good Friday) the silver casket containing the holy wood of the Cross is carried in procession. It is opened and the Title of the inscription on the Cross can be seen (Egeria)

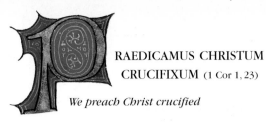 RAEDICAMUS CHRISTUM
CRUCIFIXUM (1 Cor 1, 23)

We preach Christ crucified

Celebration

The pilgrims gather in the Basilica, possibly in the chapel of the relic of the Holy Cross. The animator invites the pilgrims to recite, or sing, the following canticle (Phil 2, 6–11):

℟. Come let us adore Christ the Lord,
    at His name every knee shall bow.

Though he was in the form of God, he did not
    count equality with God a thing to be grasped. ℟.

But emptied himself, taking the form of a servant,
being born in the likeness of men. ℟.

And being found in human form he humbled himself
and became obedient unto death, even death on a
    cross. ℟.

Therefore God has highly exalted him and bestowed
    on him the name which is above every name. ℟.

That at the name of Jesus every knee should bow,
in heaven and on earth and under the earth,
and every tongue confess that Jesus Christ is Lord,
    to the glory of God the Father. ℟.

The animator recalls the meaning of the prayer to the Cross:

We know that the Cross of Christ is the chosen sign of God to show us His love. We cannot only admire it at a distance: Jesus invites us to be part of the experience of the Cross to learn how to love. This is the witness of the Saints, servants of the Gospel of the Cross of Jesus Christ.

Let us pray *(silent pause)*

Father, you wanted to save the human race by the Cross of Jesus your Son, grant to us, who have known on earth the mystery of his love, the joy of participating in heaven in the fruits of redemption. Through Christ our Lord. ℟. Amen.

The Word of God

From the First Letter of Saint Paul to the Corinthians
(1, 18.22–25)

The message of the Cross is folly for those who are on the way to ruin, but for those of us who are on the road to salvation it is the power of God.

While the Jews demand miracles and the Greeks look for wisdom, we preach Christ crucified: to the Jews an obstacle they cannot get over, to the Gentiles foolishness, but to those who have been called, whether they are Jews or Greeks, a Christ who is both the power of God and the wisdom of God. God's folly is wiser than human wisdom, and God's weakness is stronger than human strength.

Canticle   (cf. Rev 5, 9–10.12)

℟ You have saved us through the Cross, Lord Jesus.

You are worthy to take the scroll and to break its seals.

℟ You have saved us through the Cross, Lord Jesus.

Because you were sacrificed, and with your blood you bought people for God of every race, language, people and nation.

℟ You have saved us through the Cross, Lord Jesus.

And made us a kingdom of priests for God,
to rule the whole world.

℟ You have saved us through the Cross, Lord Jesus.

Worthy is the Lamb that was sacrificed to receive power, riches, wisdom, strength, honour, glory and blessing.

℟ You have saved us through the Cross, Lord Jesus.

There they crucified him (Lk 23, 33)
THE PLACE CALLED THE SKULL, Basilica of the Holy Sepulchre, Jerusalem

A reading from the Gospel according to Luke

(23, 33.39–43)

When they reached the place called The Skull, there they crucified him and the two criminals, one on his right, the other on his left. One of the criminals hanging there abused him: "Are you not the Christ? Save yourself and us as well." But the other spoke up and rebuked him. "Have you no fear of God at all?" he said. "You got the same sentence as he did, but in our case we deserved it: we are paying for what we did. But this man has done nothing wrong." Then he said, "Jesus, remember me when you come into your kingdom." He answered him, "In truth I tell you, today you will be with me in paradise."

Intercessions

In himself, Christ carried our sins on the Cross, so that free from our sins, we may give ourselves to justice. We turn to God our prayer (through the intercession of Saint Lawrence):

℟. Lord have mercy.

or Kyrie, eleison.

You went to Jerusalem to suffer death and enter into glory, guide your pilgrim Church to the Eternal Passover. ℟.

You prayed for Peter that he would not be lacking in faith, give strength and courage to the Pope in his apostolic ministry. ℟.

Your side was pierced with a lance and there came out blood and water, symbols of the sacraments of the Church, heal our wounds through the power of your grace. ℟.

They stand in line; and all bow their heads
while they first touch with their forehead and then see with
their eyes the Cross and the Title, and they kiss both (Egeria)
THE TITLE, Relic of the Passion, Santa Croce in Gerusalemme, Rome

You made out of the Cross the tree of life, give the fruit of salvation to all those who have been reborn in baptism. ℟.

From the Cross you gave as mother to your disciple your own Mother, grant that we live truly as her children. ℟.

You who from the Cross have forgiven the penitent thief, forgive also us sinners and welcome us into the heavenly Jerusalem. ℟.

Our Father.

God our Father,
in your mysterious design of salvation
you continue the passion of Jesus your Son
in the wounded members of his body, the Church,
(through the intercession of Saint Lawrence)
may we learn to accept and to serve lovingly
Christ in those who suffer.
Who lives and reigns for ever and ever. ℟. Amen.

At the end a Marian antiphon is said (pp. 235–236).

Celebration of the Mass

One of the following Masses, votive or for various occasions, can be celebrated if the liturgical norms allow it.

* For the Holy Year *(pp. 142–148).*

From the Roman Missal:

* The Triumph of the Cross.
* The Precious Blood of Christ.
* The Sacred Heart of Jesus.

From the Masses of Our Lady:

* Mary at the Foot of the Cross, I and II.
* Consecration of the Blessed Virgin Mary.

If, at the end of the Mass, the pilgrims gather in the chapel of the Holy Cross, the Intercessions *given for the above* Celebration of the Word *may be used.*

THE CATACOMBS

This celebration, having as a theme the value of Christian witness which demands "the offering of one's life to Christ", *can take place, with the necessary changes, in a church within the diocese which is dedicated to a martyr.*

Let the hosts of martyrs praise you (Te Deum)
THE MARTYRS, Sant'Apollinare Nuovo, Ravenna

BEATI QUI PERSECUTIONEM PATIUNTUR (Mt 5, 10)

Blessed are those who are persecuted

Reflection

"I only believe those stories where the witnesses are made to die." This is what Blaise Pascal wrote in his *Pensées*. He re-echoes what was written by the first Christian writers, like Saint Athanasius, Bishop of Alexandria in the fourth century, who said: "The witness given by the blood of the martyrs is clearer than any speech."

The following phrase belongs to Tertullian, an African lawyer of the third century: "The blood of the Christian is a seed." A similar thought about martyrdom sees "John the Baptist's head on the plate [as] speaking louder than when it was joined to his neck" (Primo Mazzolari).

Jesus was clear in his words when sending out his disciples. He sent them out as lambs among the wolves of hatred and evil: "Be prepared for people to hand you over to Sanhedrins and scourge you in their synagogues. You will be brought before governors and kings for my sake, as evidence to them and to the Gentiles … Do not be afraid of those who kill the body but cannot kill the soul; fear him rather who can destroy both body and soul in hell … Anyone who finds his life will lose it; anyone who loses his life for my sake will find it" (Mt 10, 17–18.28.39). "Remember the words I said to you: A servant is not greater than his master. If they persecuted me, they will persecute you too; if they keep my word, they will keep yours as well" (Jn 15, 20).

This is the way of the Cross on which the disciple has to set out, a way which is full of obstacles where one's feet will bleed, like those of Jesus on his way to Golgotha and like those of Mary, full of sorrow, she who on that hill will be crucified in her heart (Lk 2, 35). "But anybody who tries to live in devotion to Christ – this is Saint Paul's warning – is certain to be persecuted" (2 Tim 3, 12).

This is a choice which has no place for despair, as is witnessed by Jesus himself who, on the Cross, in the moment of complete abandonment, commends his life to the Father, forgiving those who were crucifying him (cf. Lk 23, 34. 46); the first Christian martyr Stephen behaves in the same way. "Christians feel invigorated, in the knowledge that they bring to the world the true light, Christ the Lord" (IM 2).

Martyrdom is an act of love, pure and total, as Christ reminded his disciples at the Last Supper: "No one can have greater love than to lay down his life for his friends" (Jn 15, 13). An act of self-giving to God and to the brethren, martyrdom – as the original Greek word denotes – is a "witness" of faith and love. This is what Saint Ignatius, Bishop of Antioch, insists on in his letters to the various Christian Churches, written while he was being taken to Rome to be thrown to wild beasts around the year 107. To the Roman Christians he writes: "I am the wheat of God, and am ground by the teeth of the wild beasts, that I may be found the pure bread of God … My love has been crucified, and there is no fire in me desiring to be fed; but there is within me a water that lives and speaks, saying to me inwardly, 'Come to the Father'." All true Christians live their daily martyrdom according to the words of Jesus: "Then, speaking to all, he said, 'If anyone wants to be a follower of mine, let him renounce himself and take up his cross every day and follow me'" (Lk 9, 23).

Paul VI writes: "It is necessary for the Church to suffer. It is for her fidelity to Christ. It is for her being authentic. It is for her being always able to speak to the world and save it. Martyrdom is one of her charisms."

Long is the line of the martyrs that from Jerusalem, from the Roman catacombs, from every corner of the earth, from "every nation, race, tribe and language", who present themselves "in front of the throne and in front of the Lamb, dressed in white robes and holding palms in their hands" (Rev 7, 9). In that group of witnesses we see the innocents whose blood marked the birth of Christ, John the Baptist and the Apostles, "glad to have had the honour of suffering humiliation for the sake of the name" (Acts 5, 41).

We see Stephen, whose death resembles that of Christ, with forgiveness to those who were persecuting him and completely trusting himself to God (cf. Acts 7, 59–60). Lawrence, Sebastian, Agatha, Cecilia, Lucy, and so many others whose names are written in that "book of life" which belongs to God. Among them we see the faces of Maximilian Kolbe, Edith Stein, Zephyrinus Gimenez Malla, Oscar Romero, African priests and bishops, the Trappist Fathers of Thiribine in Algeria and others belonging to different Christian denominations like Dietrich Bonhoeffer, others from different religions like Gandhi. In front of them all Christ advances: they have sealed their faith by offering their lives to Christ, mindful of the beatitudes received from their Master: "Blessed are those who are persecuted in the cause of uprightness: the kingdom of Heaven is theirs. Blessed are you when people abuse you and persecute you and speak all kinds of calumny against you falsely on my account. Rejoice and be glad, for your reward will be great in heaven; this is how they persecuted the prophets before you" (Mt 5, 10–12).

The Lamb will be their shepherd and will guide them to springs of living water. And God will wipe away all tears from their eyes (Rev 7, 17). Vault above the altar, San Vitale, Ravenna

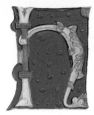 ON DILEXERUNT ANIMAM SUAM
USQUE AD MORTEM (Rev 12,11)

Giving life for Christ

Celebration

The pilgrims visiting the catacombs are invited for a moment of prayer. The animator invites the pilgrims to praise Christ and his martyrs (cf. Rev 5,9; 12, 11–12):

℟. Come let us adore the king of the martyrs,
Christ the Lord.

You are worthy to take the scroll
and to break its seals,
because you were sacrificed. ℟.

And with your blood you bought people for God
of every race, language, people and nation. ℟.

They have triumphed over him
by the blood of the Lamb
and by the word to which they bore witness. ℟.

Because even in the face of death they did not cling
to life.
So let the heavens rejoice and all who live there. ℟.

Glory. ℟.

The animator may introduce the prayer below with these words:

Taking into account the example of the martyrs of the first centuries, as well as of today's martyrs, let us renew our allegiance to Christ, always ready for people who ask us the reason for the hope that is in us.

Let us pray *(silent pause)*

O God, you enriched the first fruits of the Church in Rome
with the blood of the martyrs,
through the shining example of so many courageous
witnesses strengthen us in faith, so that we can joyfully
gather the fruits of their sacrifice.
Through Christ our Lord. ℟. Amen.

*This was the greatest love, that Stephen did not ask God
to spare him suffering but prayed that God
might forgive those who were stoning him*
(Jacobus de Voragine, *Legenda Aurea*)
SAINT STEPHEN, Fra Angelico, Nicolina Chapel, Vatican

The Word of God

From the Letter of Saint Paul to the Romans (12, 1–2)

I urge you, then, brothers, remembering the mercies of God, to offer your bodies as a living sacrifice, dedicated and acceptable to God; that is the kind of worship for you, as holy people. Do not model your behaviour on the contemporary world, but let the renewing of your minds transform you, so that you may discern for yourselves what is the will of God – what is good and acceptable and mature.

Psalm 116

℟ In you, O Lord, I put my trust.

How can I repay the Lord
for his goodness to me?
The cup of salvation I will raise;
I will call on the Lord's name. ℟

My vows to the Lord I will fulfil
before all his people.
O precious in the eyes of the Lord
is the death of his faithful. ℟

Your servant, Lord, your servant am I;
you have loosened my bonds.
A thanksgiving sacrifice I make;
I will call on the Lord's name. ℟

A reading from the Gospel according to Luke (9, 23–26)

Then, speaking to all, he said, "If anyone wants to be a follower of mine, let him renounce himself and take up his cross every day and follow me. Anyone who wants to save his life will lose it; but anyone who loses his life for my sake will save it. What benefit is it to anyone to win the whole world and forfeit or lose his very self? For if anyone is ashamed of me and of my words, of him the Son of man will be ashamed when he comes in his own glory and in the glory of the Father and the holy angels."

Lawrence said to Valerianus: "Your live coals are refreshing me."
And with a cheerful expression on his face he said to Decius:
"Look, you have burnt one side, turn to the other." Turning his
eyes to the Lord, he said: "I thank you, Lord"
(Jacobus de Voragine, *Legenda Aurea*)
SAINT LAWRENCE, Fra Angelico and School,
Nicolina Chapel, Vatican

Intercessions

United with the Saints who have been slain because of the Gospel, let us pray to our Saviour, faithful witness of God the Father. With faith we pray:

℟. You have saved us with your blood, O Lord.

For your martyrs who were not ashamed to recognize you in front of others, sustain and confirm our Pope in the mission which you have given him. ℟.

For your martyrs who have embraced death with faith, give us the true freedom of the Spirit. ℟.

For your martyrs who followed the way of the Cross, may we bear the challenges of life with fortitude. ℟.

For your martyrs who have washed their vestments with the blood of the Lamb, help us overcome the seduction of the world and the flesh. ℟.

Our Father.

The prayer of your martyrs supports us in your sight, O Father,
confirm us in a courageous adherence to the Gospel.
Through Christ our Lord. ℟. Amen.

At the end a Marian antiphon is said (pp. 235–236).

Celebration of the Mass

One of the following Masses, votive or for various occasions, can be celebrated if the liturgical norms allow it.

* For the Holy Year *(pp. 142–148)*.

From the Roman Missal:

* The Precious Blood of Christ.
* Common of Martyrs.
* For Persecuted Christians.

From the Masses of Our Lady:

* The Virgin Mary, Support and Defence of our Faith.

SANTA PUDENZIANA

SAN CLEMENTE

This celebration, having as a theme "rejoice in the Lord always", can take place, adapted as necessary, in any church within the diocese.

Born again through the Spirit
Born again to your Grace
May you be our Church
Jesus, our eternal joy!
(Roman Easter Liturgy)
MAIN APSE, Santa Pudenziana, Rome

ONSURREXISTIS CUM CHRISTO
(Col 3, 1)

Risen with Christ

Reflection

"Let us go to him, then, outside the camp, and bear his humiliation. There is no permanent city for us here; we are looking for the one which is yet to be."

These words of the Letter to the Hebrews (13, 13–14), in the form of a homily, put before our eyes the final destination towards which the pilgrim Church is heading.

Jerusalem, Rome, these shrines are only a sign pointing towards "the holy city, the new Jerusalem … He will make his home among them … He will wipe away all tears from their eyes; there will be no more death, and no more mourning or sadness or pain. The world of the past has gone" (Rev 21, 2–4).

In the Bible human history is not understood as a river which after a long and difficult journey ends up in the estuary of emptiness. That evening before he died, Jesus said: "Father, I want those you have given me to be with me where I am, so that they may always see my glory which you have given me" (Jn 17, 24).

In actual fact, when Paul writes that "the gift freely given by God is eternal life in Christ Jesus our Lord" (Rom 6, 23) he does so on the promise of Christ himself when in his speech in the synagogue of Capernaum, by the sea of Tiberias, he solemnly proclaimed: "Anyone who eats my flesh and drinks my blood has eternal life, and I shall raise that person up on the last day" (Jn 6, 54).

Amidst suffering and fear, we are on our way towards this destination, holding high the torch of hope: "Every Jubilee Year is like an invitation to a wedding feast" (IM 4).

As the Old Testament is pervaded with Messianic hope, so the New Testament and the history of the Church are sustained by the hope of Christ's coming which will give the final seal to the adventure of humanity.

It is fitting that the last words of the Bible recall this expectation: "Come, Lord Jesus: I am indeed coming soon. Amen" (Rev 22, 20). And: "when he appears we shall be like him, because we shall see him as he really is" (1 Jn 3, 2).

With the Spirit reaching out to the beatitude promised to the pure of heart (cf. Mt 5, 8), through the outward sign of the pilgrimage and the living out of life's daily demands, we become living signs of a constant hope.

This is how the French writer Gilbert Cesbron expresses the above: "We are sailing between these two reefs: his love and our freedom. It is possible to refuse love even when one is face to face with it; but the thought that divine love can refuse us and distance itself from us seems to me a sacrilege."

We are therefore not alone on this journey: "He first loved us ... it is not we who loved God, but God loved us and sent his Son to expiate our sins" (1 Jn 4, 19.10).

"History rushes forward, and God is always there", wrote Saint Hilary of Poitiers in his treatise on the Trinity (fourth century), "and it is with God that we can fully encounter that glory which is light, communion and love."

"Now we see only reflections in a mirror, mere riddles, but then we shall be seeing face to face ... This is the way we shall be with the Lord for ever ... Since you have been raised up to be with Christ" (1 Cor 13, 12; 1 Thess 4, 17; Col 3, 1).

**AUDETE IN DOMINO
SEMPER** (Phil 4, 4)

Always be joyful in the Lord

Celebration

The animator invites the pilgrims to praise Christ the Lord
(cf. Rev 19, 1–7)

℟. Servants of the Lord,
    O bless the Lord.

Salvation and glory and power belong to our God,
for his judgments are true and just. ℟.

Praise our God, all you his servants,
you who fear him, small and great. ℟.

For the Lord our God the Almighty reigns.
Let us rejoice and exult and give him the glory. ℟.

For the marriage of the Lamb has come,
and his Bride has made herself ready. ℟.

Glory. ℟.

*The animator may introduce the prayer below with these
words:*

The Jubilee is a time for joy: the joy of salvation, of
forgiveness, of brotherhood that accompanies the
pilgrimage of the believers towards the happiness of
the kingdom of heaven, where God will wipe away
every tear from their eyes (cf. Rev 21,4). Let us pray
to God, in this basilica (through the intercession of
Saint Clement), for grace to live in the Christian joy.

Let us pray *(silent pause)*

Through the strength of your love,
sustain, O Lord, our pilgrimage towards Christ;
and with patient perseverance
may we mature in faith
and accept with thanksgiving
the joy that your Gospel brings.
Through Christ our Lord. ℟. Amen.

112

The Word of God

From the First Letter of Saint Paul to the Thessalonians
(5, 16–24)

Rejoice always, pray constantly, give thanks in all circumstances; for this is the will of God in Christ Jesus for you. Do not quench the Spirit, do not despise prophesying, but test everything; hold fast what is good, abstain from every form of evil. May the God of peace himself sanctify you wholly; and may your spirit and soul and body be kept sound and blameless at the coming of our Lord Jesus Christ. He who calls you is faithful, and he will do it.

Psalm 103

℟ Blessed be the Lord, source of happiness.

My soul, give thanks to the Lord,
all my being, bless his holy name.
My soul, give thanks to the Lord
and never forget all his blessings. ℟

It is he who forgives all your guilt,
who heals every one of your ills,
who redeems your life from the grave,
who crowns you with love and compassion. ℟

A reading from the Gospel according to John (15, 5–11)

Whoever remains in me, with me in him, bears fruit in plenty; for cut off from me you can do nothing. Anyone who does not remain in me is thrown away like a branch – and withers; these branches are collected and thrown on the fire and are burnt. If you remain in me and my words remain in you, you may ask for whatever you please and you will get it. It is to the glory of my Father that you should bear much fruit and be my disciples. I have loved you just as the Father has loved me. Remain in my love. If you keep my commandments you will remain in my love, just as I have kept my Father's commandments and remain in his love. I have told you this so that my own joy may be in you and your joy be complete.

He loves us and has washed away our sins
with his blood, and made us a Kingdom of Priests
to serve his God and Father; to him, then, be glory
and power for ever and ever (Rev 1, 5–6)
MAIN APSE, San Clemente, Rome

IN MEMORIAM

John Cardinal O'Connor
1920 – 2000

+ + + + +

Born:	January 15, 1920
Ordained a Priest of God:	December 15, 1945
Episcopal Ordination:	May 27, 1979
Bishop of Scranton:	June 29, 1983
Archbishop of New York:	March 19, 1984
Invested as Cardinal:	May 25, 1985
Entered into Eternal Life:	May 3, 2000

All-powerful Father, God of Mercy,
You gave to Cardinal O'Connor,
Your servant,
the dignity of the priesthood and
the privilege of doing
the work of Christ on earth.
May he now rejoice in the fellowship
of the successors of the Apostles
whose office he shared in this life.
bring him to eternal life with Christ
in heaven
Who is Lord forever and ever.
Amen.

THERE CAN BE NO LOVE WITHOUT JUSTICE

"I find myself in unutterable peace, a peace born of
the grace of God, and of the goodness of God's
people. Life is such a gift and after almost eighty
years of living it, I have no sentiment so strong as
gratitude . . ."

Cardinal O'Connor
August 30, 1999

The animator may briefly address those present, or read out the following passage from the Apostolic Exhortation Gaudete in Domino, *written by Paul VI on the occasion of the 1975 Holy Year.*

Paschal joy is not just that of a possible transfiguration: it is the joy of the new presence of the Risen Christ dispensing to his own the Holy Spirit, so that he may dwell with them. The Holy Spirit is given to the Church as the inexhaustible principle of her joy as the bride of the glorified Christ. He recalls to her mind, through the ministry of grace and truth exercised by the successors of the Apostles, the very teaching of the Lord. The Holy Spirit stirs up in the Church divine life and the apostolate. And the Christian knows that this Spirit will never be quenched in the course of history. The source of hope manifested at Pentecost will never be exhausted.

Intercessions

To Christ, true source of happiness for all who believe in him, let us present our prayer, saying:

℟ Fill us with your joy, O Lord.

Eternal Word, you were in the beginning before anything was made, be the saviour of us all. ℟

Creator of the universe and of all those who live, be the guardian of your creation. ℟

God with us, you wanted to be like us, come and free us from the power of death. ℟

Saviour of the world who died on the Cross so that we can live, may we partake of your divine nature. ℟

Glorious Lord, who calls each one to share in the joy of your kingdom, may your face shine on our sisters and brothers whom you have already called to yourself. ℟

Our Father.

Father, source of life and joy, renew us through the strength of your Holy Spirit, that we may walk the way of your commandments and be a sign to all and bearers to all of the good news of our Saviour, your Son, Jesus Christ, who lives and reigns with you and the Holy Spirit, for ever and ever. ℟ Amen.

At the end a Marian antiphon is said (pp. 235–236).

Celebration of the Mass

One of the following Masses, votive or for various occasions, can be celebrated if the liturgical norms allow it.

* For the Holy Year *(pp. 142–148).*

From the Roman Missal:

* The Holy Spirit.
* In Thanksgiving.

From the Masses of Our Lady:

* The Virgin Mary cause of our Joy.

III
CELEBRATIONS, PRAYERS AND SONGS

The Mother of Jesus: image and beginning of the Church; she, that with her prayer helped the first fruits of the Church, intercedes with her Son (LG 68–69)
APSE, Saint Sophia, Kiev

A great crowd from every nation, race, people and language.
The Lamb will be their Shepherd (Rev 7, 9)

The Blessing of Pilgrims

So that the pilgrims will experience fully the good effects of their pilgrimage, it will be useful to arrange a special celebration for the blessing of the pilgrims at their departure or on their return. If the pilgrimage begins or ends with the celebration of Mass or the liturgy of the hours, the celebration may be concluded with a blessing of the pilgrims taken from the following texts. The present rite may be used by a priest or deacon. While maintaining the structure and chief elements of the rite, the celebrant should adapt the celebration to the circumstances of the place and the people involved.

The blessing of the pilgrims on their departure

Introductory Rites

When the group of pilgrims has gathered, a psalm or some other suitable song may be sung. After the singing, the celebrant says:

In the name of the Father, and of the Son, and of the Holy Spirit.

All make the sign of the cross and reply: Amen.

Greeting

The celebrant greets those present in the following or other suitable words, taken mainly from sacred Scripture:

May God, our strength and salvation, be with you all.

℟ And also with you.

Introductory Words

In the following or similar words, the celebrant prepares those present for the blessing:

Brothers and sisters, as we set out we should remind ourselves of the reasons for our resolve to go on this holy Jubilee pilgrimage. The holy places we intend to visit remind us that we are to renew our Christian way of life and so make our hearts a worthy dwelling place for God. We shall have the joy of meeting many of our brothers and sisters within whom we share the grace of our faith in Jesus Christ. We must show them our example of faith, hope, and love. In this way both they and we will be enriched by the help we give each other, to the praise and glory of the Most Holy Trinity.

Reading of the Word of God

A passage of holy scripture is read, followed by a psalm or hymn:

Brothers and sisters, listen to the words of the Holy Gospel according to Luke: (24, 13–35)

That very day two of them were going to a village named Emmaus, about seven miles from Jerusalem, and talking with each other about all these things that had happened.

While they were talking and discussing together, Jesus himself drew near and went with them. But their eyes were kept from recognizing him. And he said to them, "What is this conversation which you are holding with each other as you walk?" And they stood still, looking sad. Then one of them, named Cleopas, answered him, "Are you the only visitor to Jerusalem who does not know the things that have happened there in these days?"

And he said to them, "What things?" And they said to him, "Concerning Jesus of Nazareth, who was a prophet mighty in deed and word before God and all the people, and how our chief priests and rulers delivered him up to be condemned to death, and crucified him. But we had hoped that he was the one to redeem Israel. Yes, and besides all this, it is now the third day since this happened. Moreover, some women of our company amazed us. They were at the tomb early in the morning and did not find his body; and they came back saying that they had even seen a vision of angels, who said that he was alive. Some of those who were with us went to the tomb, and found it just as the women had said; but him they did not see."

And he said to them, "O foolish men, and slow of heart to believe all that the prophets have spoken! Was it not necessary that the Christ should suffer these things and enter into his glory?" And beginning with Moses and all the prophets, he interpreted to them in all the scriptures the things concerning himself.

So they drew near to the village to which they were going. He appeared to be going further, but they constrained him, saying, "Stay with us, for it is toward evening and the day is now far spent." So he went in to stay with them. When he was at table with them, he took the bread and blessed, and broke it, and gave it to them.

And their eyes were opened and they recognized him; and he vanished out of their sight. They said to each other, "Did not our hearts burn within us while he talked to us on the road, while he opened to us the scriptures?" And they rose that same hour and returned to Jerusalem; and they found the eleven gathered together and those who were with them, who said, "The Lord has risen indeed, and has appeared to Simon!" Then they told what had happened on the road, and how he was known to them in the breaking of the bread.

The celebrant may give those present a brief explanation of the biblical text, so that they may understand through faith the meaning of the celebration.

Intercessions

The intercessions are then said. Other intentions that apply to the particular circumstances may be composed.

God is the beginning and the end of life's pilgrimage. Let us call on him with confidence, saying:

℟ Lord, be the companion of our journey.

Father all-holy, of old you made yourself the guide and the way for your people as they wandered in the desert; be our protection as we begin this journey, so that we may return home again in safety.

℟. Lord, be the companion of our journey.

You have given us your only Son to be our way to you; make us follow him faithfully and unswervingly. ℟.

You gave us the Blessed Virgin Mary as the image and model for following Christ; grant that through her example we may live a new life. ℟.

You guide your pilgrim Church on earth through the Holy Spirit; may we seek you in all things and walk always in the way of your commandments. ℟.

Our Father.

Prayer of Blessing

With hands outstretched, the celebrant continues with the prayer of blessing:

All-powerful God, you always show mercy toward those who love you and you are never far away for those who seek you. Remain with your servants on this holy pilgrimage and guide their way in accordance with your will. Shelter them with your protection by day, give them the light of your grace by night, and, as their companion on the journey, bring them to their destination in safety. We ask this through Christ our Lord. ℟. Amen.

Concluding Rite

The celebrant concludes the rite by saying:

May the Lord guide us and direct our journey in safety. ℟. Amen.

May the Lord be our companion along the way. ℟. Amen.

May the Lord grant that the journey we begin, relying on him, will end happily through his protection. ℟. Amen.

The celebration can end with a suitable hymn or sacred song.

*Walk the whole way along the way that the Lord, your God,
has shown you* (Deut 5, 33)

The blessing of pilgrims after their return

Introductory Rites

When the group of pilgrims has gathered, a suitable song may be sung. After the singing, the celebrant says:

In the name of the Father, and of the Son, and of the Holy Spirit.
All make the sign of the cross and reply:
℟ Amen.

Greeting

The celebrant greets those present in the following or other suitable words:

May God, our hope and our strength, fill you with peace and with joy in the Holy Spirit.
℟ Amen.

Introductory Words

In the following or similar words, the celebrant prepares those present for the blessing:

We glorify God, Father, Son and Holy Spirit, that with the Jubilee of the year 2000 gives us a special time of grace.

We have visited the holy places, which urge us to persevere in renewing our daily life.
Coming back home, to our parishes, we, confirmed in the apostolic faith, must live according to our vocation, by virtue of which we are the chosen people of God.

He has given us the mission to announce the power of Christ, the only Saviour of the world, yesterday, today and for ever.

Reading of the Word of God

A reader, another person present, or the celebrant reads a text of sacred Scripture:

Brothers and sisters, listen to the word of God in the Letter of Saint Paul to the Ephesians   (3, 14–19)

For this reason I bow my knees before the Father, from whom every family in heaven and on earth is named, that according to the riches of his glory he may grant you to be strengthened with might through his Spirit in the inner man, and that Christ may dwell in your hearts through faith; that you, being rooted and grounded in love, may have power to comprehend with all the saints what is the breadth and length and height and depth, and to know the love of Christ which surpasses knowledge, that you may be filled with all the fullness of God.

As circumstances suggest, the celebrant may give those present a brief explanation of the biblical text, so that they may understand through faith the meaning of the celebration.

Intercessions

The intercessions are then said. Other intentions that apply to the particular circumstances may be added.

The Lord of heaven willed that in Christ's humanity the fullness of divinity should dwell as in its temple. Let us pray to him, saying

℟. Look down from heaven, O Lord, and bless your people.

Father all-holy, in the Passover exodus you prefigured the blessed road of your people toward salvation; grant that in all the paths we follow we may remain wholeheartedly faithful to you. ℟.

You have told us that here we have no lasting city; grant that we may always seek the city that is to come. ℟.

You teach all the faithful to perceive the signs of your presence along all the pathways of life; grant that like the disciples of Emmaus we may come to recognize Christ as the companion of our journey and know him in the breaking of the bread.

℟ Look down from heaven, O Lord, and bless your people.

All recite the Lord's Prayer:
Our Father.

Prayer of Blessing

With hands outstretched, the celebrant continues with the prayer of blessing:

Blessed are you, O God, Father of our Lord Jesus Christ. From all races of the earth you have chosen a people dedicated to you, eager to do what is right. Your grace has moved the hearts of these, your friends, to love you more deeply and to serve you more generously. We ask you to bless them, so that they may tell of your wonderful deeds and give proof of them in their lives. We ask this through Christ our Lord. ℟ Amen.

Concluding Rite

The celebrant concludes the rite by saying:

May God, the Lord of heaven and earth, who so graciously has accompanied you on this pilgrimage, continue to keep you under his protection. ℟ Amen.

May God, who gathered all his scattered children in Christ Jesus, grant that you will be of one heart and one mind in Christ. ℟ Amen.

May God, whose goodness inspires in you all that you desire and achieve, strengthen your devotion by his blessing. ℟ Amen.

The celebration may conclude with a suitable song.

*Glory to you, Source of the Son! Glory to you, beauty of the
Father! Glory to you, Spirit of the Son and Father!*
(Synesius of Cyrene, *Hymn to Christ*)
<small>REVELATION OF THE HOLY TRINITY, A. Rublev,
Monastery of Saint Sergius, Russia</small>

The Order of Mass

In the sign of consecrated bread and wine, Jesus Christ, risen and glorified, the Light of all peoples (cf. Lk 2, 32), reveals the ongoing work of his Incarnation. He remains alive and real among us to feed the faithful with his Body and his Blood (IM 11)

RITUS INITIALES

Cantus ad introitum

In nomine Patris, et Filii, et Spiritus Sancti.
℟ *Amen.*

Salutatio populi

Dominus vobiscum.
℟ *Et cum spiritu tuo.*

Actus paenitentialis

Fratres, agnoscamus peccata nostra, ut apti simus ad sacra mysteria celebranda.

Confiteor Deo omnipotenti, et vobis, fratres, quia peccavi nimis cogitatione, verbo, opere et omissione (percutientes sibi pectus)*: mea culpa, mea culpa, mea maxima culpa. Ideo precor beatam Mariam semper Virginem, omnes Angelos et Sanctos, et vos, fratres, orare pro me ad Dominum Deum nostrum.*

INTRODUCTORY RITES

Entrance Song

In the name of the Father, and of the Son and of the Holy Spirit.
℟ Amen.

Greeting

The Lord be with you.
℟ And also with you.

Penitential Rite

My brothers and sisters, to prepare ourselves to celebrate the sacred mysteries, let us call to mind our sins.

I confess to almighty God, and to you, my brothers and sisters, that I have sinned through my own fault in my thoughts and in my words, in what I have done, and in what I have failed to do. And I ask blessed Mary, ever virgin, all the angels and saints, and you, my brothers and sisters, to pray for me to the Lord our God.

Misereatur nostri omnipotens Deus, et, dimissis peccatis nostris, perducat nos ad vitam aeternam. ℟ *Amen.*

May almighty God have mercy on us, forgive us our sins, and bring us to everlasting life. ℟ *Amen.*

Kyrie, eleison

Kyrie, eleison.
℟ *Kyrie, eleison.*

Christe, eleison.
℟ *Christe, eleison.*

Kyrie, eleison
℟ *Kyrie, eleison.*

Lord, Have Mercy

Lord, have mercy.
℟ Lord, have mercy.

Christ, have mercy.
℟ Christ, have mercy.

Lord, have mercy.
℟ Lord, have mercy.

Gloria in excelsis

Gloria in excelsis Deo et in terra pax hominibus bonae voluntatis. Laudamus te, benedicimus te, adoramus te, glorificamus te, gratias agimus tibi propter magnam gloriam tuam, Domine Deus, Rex caelestis, Deus Pater omnipotens.
Domine Fili unigenite, Iesu Christe, Domine Deus, Agnus Dei, Filius Patris, qui tollis peccata mundi, miserere nobis; qui tollis peccata mundi, suscipe deprecationem nostram. Qui sedes ad dexteram Patris, miserere nobis. Quoniam tu solus Sanctus, tu solus Dominus, tu solus Altissimus, Iesu Christe, cum Sancto Spiritu: in gloria Dei Patris. Amen.

Gloria

Glory to God in the highest, and peace to his people on earth.

Lord God, heavenly King, almighty God and Father, we worship you, we give you thanks, we praise you for your glory.

Lord Jesus Christ, only Son of the Father, Lord God, Lamb of God, you take away the sin of the world: have mercy on us; you are seated at the right hand of the Father: receive our prayer.

For you alone are the Holy One, you alone are the Lord, you alone are the Most High, Jesus Christ, with the Holy Spirit, in the glory of God the Father.
Amen.

Collecta

Opening Prayer

The Angels Sing Glory to god, Benozzo Gozzoli, Palazzo Medici Riccardi, Florence

Liturgia Verbi | Liturgy of the Word

Lectiones | Readings

Verbum Domini.
℟. *Deo gratias.*

This is the word of the Lord.
℟. Thanks be to God.

Evangelium | Gospel

Dominus vobiscum.
℟. *Et cum spiritu tuo.*

The Lord be with you.
℟. And also with you.

Lectio sancti Evangelii secundum N.
℟. *Gloria tibi, Domine.*

A reading from the holy gospel according to N.
℟. Glory to you, Lord.

Finito Evangelio:
Verbum Domini.
℟. *Laus tibi, Christe.*

At the end:
This is the gospel of the Lord.
℟. Praise to you, Lord Jesus Christ.

Homilia | Homily

Professio Fidei | The Profession of Faith

Credo in unum Deum, Patrem omnipotentem, factorem caeli et terrae, visibilium omnium et invisibilium.

Et in unum Dominum Iesum Christum, Filium Dei unigenitum, et ex Patre natum ante omnia saecula. Deum de Deo, lumen de lumine, Deum verum de Deo vero, genitum, non factum, consubstantialem Patri: per quem omnia facta sunt. Qui propter nos homines et

We believe in one God, the Father, the Almighty, maker of heaven and earth, of all that is seen and unseen.

We believe in one Lord, Jesus Christ, the only Son of God, eternally begotten of the Father, God from God, Light from Light, true God from true God, begotten, not made, one in being with the Father. Through him all things were made. For us men and for our salvation he came down from heaven: by

propter nostram salutem descendit de caelis. Et incarnatus est de Spiritu Sancto ex Maria Virgine, et homo factus est. Crucifixus etiam pro nobis sub Pontio Pilato; passus et sepultus est, et resurrexit tertia die, secundum Scripturas, et ascendit in caelum, sedet ad dexteram Patris. Et iterum venturus est cum gloria iudicare vivos et mortuos, cuius regni non erit finis.

Et in Spiritum Sanctum, Dominum et vivificantem: qui ex Patre Filioque procedit. Qui cum Patre et Filio simul adoratur et conglorificatur: qui locutus est per prophetas. Et unam, sanctam, catholicam et apostolicam Ecclesiam. Confiteor unum baptisma in remissionem peccatorum. Et exspecto resurrectionem mortuorum, et vitam venturi saeculi. Amen.

the power of the Holy Spirit he was born of the Virgin Mary, and became man. For our sake he was crucified under Pontius Pilate; he suffered, died, and was buried. On the third day he rose again in fulfilment of the Scriptures; he ascended into heaven and is seated at the right hand of the Father. He will come again in glory to judge the living and the dead, and his kingdom will have no end.

We believe in the Holy Spirit, the Lord, the giver of life, who proceeds from the Father and the Son. With the Father and the Son he is worshipped and glorified. He has spoken through the Prophets.

We believe in one holy catholic and apostolic Church. We acknowledge one baptism for the forgiveness of sins. We look for the resurrection of the dead, and the life of the world to come. Amen.

Oratio universalis

General Intercessions

LITURGIA EUCHARISTICA

Praeparatio donorum

Benedictus es, Domine, Deus universi, quia de tua largitate accepimus panem, quem tibi offerimus, fructum terrae et operis manuum hominum, ex quo nobis fiet panis vitae.

℟ *Benedictus Deus in saecula.*

Benedictus es, Domine, Deus universi, quia de tua largitate accepimus vinum, quod tibi offerimus, fructum vitis et operis manuum hominum, ex quo nobis fiet potus spiritalis.

℟ *Benedictus Deus in saecula.*

Orate, fratres: ut meum ac vestrum sacrificium acceptabile fiat apud Deum Patrem omnipotentem.

℟ *Suscipiat Dominus sacrificium de manibus tuis ad laudem et gloriam nominis sui, ad utilitatem quoque nostram totiusque Ecclesiae suae sanctae.*

Oratio super oblata

LITURGY OF THE EUCHARIST

Preparation of the Gifts

Blessed are you, Lord, God of all creation. Through your goodness we have this bread to offer, which earth has given and human hands have made. It will become for us the bread of life.

℟ Blessed be God for ever.

Blessed are you, Lord, God of all creation. Through your goodness we have this wine to offer, fruit of the vine and work of human hands. It will become our spiritual drink.

℟ Blessed be God for ever.

Pray, brethren, that my sacrifice and yours may be acceptable to God, the almighty Father.

℟ May the Lord accept the sacrifice at your hands for the praise and glory of his name, for our good, and the good of all his Church.

Prayer over the Gifts

All life, all holiness comes from you by the working of the Holy Spirit
"GLORY" WINDOW IN THE APSE, Bernini, Saint Peter's, Rome

PREX EUCHARISTICA

Dominus vobiscum.
℟. *Et cum spiritu tuo.*

Sursum corda.
℟. *Habemus ad Dominum.*

Gratias agamus Domino Deo nostro.
℟. *Dignum et iustum est.*

EUCHARISTIC PRAYER

The Lord be with you.
℟. And also with you.

Lift up your hearts.
℟. We lift them up to the Lord.

Let us give thanks to the Lord our God.
℟. It is right to give him thanks and praise.

Praefatio

Sanctus

Sanctus, Sanctus, Sanctus Dominus Deus Sabaoth. Pleni sunt caeli et terra gloria tua. Hosanna in excelsis. Benedictus qui venit in nomine Domini. Hosanna in excelsis.

Prex Eucharistica III

Vere Sanctus es, Domine, et merito te laudat omnis a te condita creatura, quia per Filium tuum, Dominum nostrum Iesum Christum, Spiritus Sancti operante virtute, vivificas et sanctificas universa, et populum tibi congregare non desinis, ut a solis ortu usque ad occasum oblatio munda offeratur nomini tuo.

Supplices ergo te, Domine, deprecamur, ut haec munera, quae tibi sacranda detulimus, eodem Spiritu sanctificare digneris, ut Corpus et Sanguis fiant Filii tui Domini nostri Iesu Christi, cuius mandato haec mysteria celebramus.

Ipse enim in qua nocte tradebatur accepit panem et tibi gratias agens benedixit, fregit, deditque discipulis suis, dicens: Accipite et manducate ex hoc omnes: hoc est enim

Preface

Sanctus

Holy, holy, holy Lord, God of power and might, heaven and earth are full of your glory. Hosanna in the highest. Blessed is he who comes in the name of the Lord. Hosanna in the highest.

Eucharistic Prayer III

Father, you are holy indeed, and all creation rightly gives you praise. All life, all holiness comes from you through your Son, Jesus Christ our Lord, by the working of the Holy Spirit. From age to age you gather a people to yourself, so that from east to west a perfect offering may be made to the glory of your name.

And so, Father, we bring you these gifts. We ask you to make them holy by the power of your Spirit, that they may become the body and blood of your Son, our Lord Jesus Christ, at whose command we celebrate this eucharist.

On the night he was betrayed, he took bread and gave you thanks and praise. He broke the bread, gave it to his disciples and said: Take this, all of you, and eat it: this

Corpus meum, quod pro vobis tradetur.

is my body which will be given up for you.

Simili modo, postquam cenatum est, accipiens calicem, et tibi gratias agens benedixit, deditque discipulis suis dicens: **Accipite et bibite ex eo omnes: hic est enim calix Sanguinis mei novi et aeterni testamenti, qui pro vobis et pro multis effundetur in remissionem peccatorum. Hoc facite in meam commemorationem.**

When supper was ended, he took the cup. Again he gave you thanks and praise, gave the cup to his disciples, and said: **Take this, all of you, and drink from it: this is the cup of my blood, the blood of the new and everlasting covenant. It will be shed for you and for all, so that sins may be forgiven. Do this in memory of me.**

*M*ysterium fidei.

Let us proclaim the mystery of faith.

℟. *Mortem tuam annuntiamus, Domine, et tuam resurrectionem confitemur, donec venias.*

℟. Christ has died,
Christ is risen,
Christ will come again.

*M*emores igitur, Domine, eiusdem Filii tui salutiferae passionis necnon mirabilis resurrectionis et ascensionis in caelum, sed et praestolantes alterum eius adventum, offerimus tibi, gratias referentes, hoc sacrificium vivum et sanctum.

Father, calling to mind the death your Son endured for our salvation, his glorious resurrection and ascension into heaven, and ready to greet him when he comes again, we offer you in thanksgiving this holy and living sacrifice.

Respice, quaesumus, in oblationem Ecclesiae tuae et, agnoscens Hostiam, cuius voluisti immolatione placari, concede, ut qui Corpore et Sanguine Filii tui reficimur, Spiritu eius Sancto repleti, unum corpus et unus spiritus inveniamur in Christo.

Look with favour on your Church's offering, and see the Victim whose death has reconciled us to yourself. Grant that we, who are nourished by his body and blood, may be filled with his Holy Spirit, and become one body, one spirit in Christ.

Ipse nos tibi perficiat munus aeternum, ut cum electis tuis hereditatem consequi valeamus, in primis cum beatissima Virgine, Dei Genetrice, Maria, cum beatis Apostolis tuis et gloriosis Martyribus (cum Sancto N.: Sancto diei vel patrono*) et omnibus Sanctis, quorum intercessione perpetuo apud te confidimus adiuvari.*

May he make us an everlasting gift to you and enable us to share in the inheritance of your saints, with Mary, the virgin Mother of God; with the apostles, the martyrs, (Saint N.) and all your saints, on whose constant intercession we rely for help.

Haec Hostia nostrae reconciliationis proficiat, quaesumus, Domine, ad totius mundi pacem atque salutem. Ecclesiam tuam, peregrinantem in terra, in fide et caritate firmare digneris cum famulo tuo Papa nostro N. et Episcopo nostro N., cum episcopali ordine et universo clero et omni populo acquisitionis tuae.

Lord, may this sacrifice, which has made our peace with you, advance the peace and salvation of all the world. Strengthen in faith and love your pilgrim Church on earth; your servant, Pope N., our bishop N., and all the bishops, with the clergy and the entire people your Son has gained for you.

Votis huius familiae, quam tibi astare voluisti, adesto propitius. Omnes filios tuos ubique dispersos tibi, clemens Pater, miseratus coniunge.
Fratres nostros defunctos et omnes qui, tibi placentes, ex hoc saeculo transierunt, in regnum tuum benignus admitte, ubi fore speramus, ut simul gloria tua perenniter satiemur, per Christum Dominum nostrum, per quem mundo bona cuncta largiris.

Father, hear the prayers of the family you have gathered here before you. In mercy and love unite all your children wherever they may be.

Welcome into your kingdom our departed brothers and sisters, and all who have left this world in your friendship. We hope to enjoy for ever the vision of your glory, through Christ our Lord, from whom all good things come.

Per ipsum, et cum ipso, et in ipso, est tibi Deo Patri omnipotenti, in unitate Spiritus Sancti, omnis honor et gloria per omnia saecula saeculorum. R. Amen.

Through him, with him, in him, in the unity of the Holy Spirit, all glory and honour is yours, almighty Father, for ever and ever.
R. Amen.

RITUS COMMUNIONIS

COMMUNION RITE

Oratio dominica

Lord's Prayer

Praeceptis salutaribus moniti, et divina institutione formati, audemus dicere:

Let us pray with confidence to the Father in the words our Saviour gave us:

Omnes:

All:

Pater noster, qui es in caelis: sanctificetur nomen tuum; adveniat regnum tuum; fiat voluntas tua, sicut in caelo, et in terra. Panem nostrum cotidianum da nobis hodie; et dimitte nobis debita nostra, sicut et nos dimittimus debitoribus nostris; et ne nos inducas in tentationem; sed libera nos a malo.

Our Father, who art in heaven, hallowed be thy name; thy kingdom come; thy will be done on earth as it is in heaven. Give us this day our daily bread; and forgive us our trespasses as we forgive those who trespass against us; and lead us not into temptation, but deliver us from evil.

Libera nos, quaesumus, Domine, ab omnibus malis, da propitius pacem in diebus nostris, ut, ope misericordiae tuae adiuti, et a peccato simus semper liberi et ab omni perturbatione securi: exspectantes beatam spem et adventum Salvatoris nostri Iesu Christi.

Deliver us, Lord, from every evil, and grant us peace in our day. In your mercy keep us free from sin and protect us from all anxiety, as we wait in joyful hope for the coming of our Saviour, Jesus Christ.

R. Quia tuum est regnum, et potestas, et gloria in saecula.

R. For the kingdom, the power, and the glory are yours, now and for ever.

Ritus pacis

Domine Iesu Christe, qui dixisti Apostolis tuis: pacem relinquo vobis, pacem meam do vobis: ne respicias peccata nostra, sed fidem Ecclesiae tuae; eamque secundum voluntatem tuam pacificare et coadunare digneris. Qui vivis et regnas in saecula saeculorum.

℟ *Amen.*

Pax Domini sit semper vobiscum.

℟ *Et cum spiritu tuo.*

Offerte vobis pacem.

Agnus Dei

Agnus Dei, qui tollis peccata mundi: miserere nobis.

Agnus Dei, qui tollis peccata mundi: miserere nobis.

Agnus Dei, qui tollis peccata mundi: dona nobis pacem.

Communio

Ecce Agnus Dei, ecce qui tollit peccata mundi. Beati qui ad cenam Agni vocati sunt.

℟ *Domine, non sum dignus, ut intres sub tectum meum: sed tantum dic verbo, et sanabitur anima mea.*

Sign of Peace

Lord Jesus Christ, you said to your apostles: I leave you peace, my peace I give you. Look not on our sins, but on the faith of your Church, and grant us the peace and unity of your kingdom where you live for ever and ever.

℟ Amen.

The peace of the Lord be with you always.

℟ And also with you.

Let us offer each other the sign of peace.

Breaking of the Bread

Lamb of God, you take away the sins of the world, have mercy on us.

Lamb of God, you take away the sins of the world, have mercy on us.

Lamb of God, you take away the sins of the world, grant us peace.

Communion

This is the Lamb of God who takes away the sins of the world. Happy are those who are called to his supper.

℟ Lord, I am not worthy to receive you, but only say the word and I shall be healed.

Corpus Christi.	The body of Christ.
℟ *Amen.*	℟ Amen.
Cantus ad Communionem	Communion Antiphon or Hymn
Oratio post Communionem	Prayer after Communion

Ritus conclusionis	**Concluding rite**
Dominus vobiscum.	The Lord be with you.
℟ *Et cum spiritu tuo.*	℟ And also with you.
Benedicat vos omnipotens Deus, Pater, et Filius, et Spiritus Sanctus.	May almighty God bless you, the Father, and the Son, and the Holy Spirit.
℟ *Amen.*	℟ Amen.
Ite, Missa est.	The Mass is ended; go in peace.
℟ *Deo gratias.*	℟ Thanks be to God.

CORONATION OF THE VIRGIN, Fra Angelico, Uffizi, Florence

Various Masses

The texts are given of Masses which are suitable for use during the Jubilee pilgrimage. They are to be used only when such Masses are allowed by liturgical law.

MASS FOR THE HOLY YEAR

I.

Entrance Antiphon (Ps 89, 1–2)

Lord, you have been our dwelling place in all generations; from everlasting to everlasting you are God.

Easter: Alleluia.

Opening Prayer

O God, who in the fullness of time
sent your Son into the world as our Saviour,
grant, we pray, that all those who journey as pilgrims in this world
may be led to you by the light of his Paschal Mystery,
who lives and reigns with you…

℟ Amen.

First Reading (Is 61, 1–3.6.8)

The spirit of Lord has been given to me, for he has anointed me. He has sent me to bring good news to the poor, to bind up hearts that are broken; to proclaim liberty to captives, freedom to those in prison; to proclaim a year of favour from the Lord, a day of vengeance for our God, to comfort all those who mourn and give to them for ashes a garland; for mourning robe the oil of gladness, for despondency, praise. You will be named "priests of the Lord", they will call you "ministers of our God". I reward them faithfully and make an everlasting covenant with them.

Easter: First Reading 1 Peter 2, 4–5.9–10 *(see p. 40)*

Responsorial Psalm
Psalm 67 *(see p. 51)*

Gospel Acclamation
Alleluia.
Jesus Christ, the first-born of the dead,
to you be glory and power for ever and ever.

Gospel

Listen to the words of the Holy Gospel according to Luke (Lk 4, 16–21)

Jesus came to Nazareth, where he had been brought up, and went into the synagogue on the Sabbath day as he usually did. He stood up to read, and they handed him the scroll of the prophet Isaiah. Unrolling the scroll he found the place where it is written:
The spirit of the Lord has been given to me,
for he has anointed me.
He has sent me to bring the good news to the poor
to proclaim liberty to captives
and to the blind new sight
and to set the downtrodden free,
to proclaim the Lord's year of favour.
He then rolled up the scroll, gave it back to the assistant and sat down. And all eyes in the synagogue were fixed on him. Then he began to speak to them, "This text is being fulfilled today even as you listen".

or: Matthew 5, 1–12 *(see p. 167)*
  Matthew 28, 16–20 *(see p. 56)*

Intercessions *(see pp. 42, 56, 70)*

Prayer over the Gifts

Lord, may the offering that we present
on your altars in joyful celebration of this holy year
be acceptable in your sight,
so that we may come to share in the eternal life
of Him by whose mortality we are saved from death,
Jesus Christ our Lord,
who lives...

℟ Amen.

Preface

The Lord be with you.
℟ And also with you.

Lift up your hearts.
℟ We lift them up to the Lord.

Let us give thanks to the Lord our God.
℟ It is right to give him thanks and praise.

It is truly right and just, our duty and our salvation
always and everywhere to give you thanks, O Lord,
Father most holy, almighty and eternal God:
through Christ our Lord.
Begotten as your Son before all ages,
he was born in time of the Virgin Mary
and anointed by the Holy Spirit.
In your name he proclaimed a time of grace
bringing consolation to the afflicted, redemption to
    captives,
salvation and peace to the whole human race.
Truly he himself embodies the new creation
that shines forth in every age,
surpassing every human hope.
And so, with countless Angels,
with one voice we lift up our praise to you, as we say:

Holy, holy, holy Lord, God of power and might ...

Communion Antiphon (Heb 13, 8)

Jesus Christ is the same yesterday, today and for ever.

Easter: Alleluia.

Prayer after Communion

Lord, may our sharing at your table make us holy,
and grant that through the mystery of your Church
all nations may receive with joy
the salvation which your only-begotten Son
accomplished on the cross.
Through Christ …

℟ Amen.

Solemn Blessing

May the Lord bless you and keep you.

℟ Amen.

May he make his countenance to shine upon you
and show you his mercy.

℟ Amen.

May he turn his face to you and give you his peace.

℟ Amen.

And may the blessing of almighty God,
the Father, and the Son, + and the Holy Spirit,
descend upon you and remain for ever.

℟ Amen.

II.

Entrance Antiphon (Rev 19, 5; 12, 10)

Praise our God,
all you who fear him,
small and great,
for now the salvation …
Easter: Alleluia.

Opening Prayer

O God, who through your only-begotten Son
brought to the human race
the remedy of salvation and the gift of eternal life,
grant to all who are reborn in Christ
the desire and the strength to do what you
    command
so that the people called to your kingdom
may be united in faith and in holiness of life.
Through Christ …

℟. Amen.

First Reading
Isaiah 61, 1–3.6.8 *(see p. 142)*

Responsorial Psalm
Psalm 67 *(see p. 51)*

Gospel
Luke 4, 16–21 *(see p. 143)*

Intercessions *(see pp. 42, 56, 70)*

Prayer over the Gifts

Lord, look upon the face of your Christ,
who gave himself as a ransom for all,
so that through him from the rising of the sun to its
    setting
your name may be exalted among the nations,
and one single offering may be presented to your
    majesty in every place.
Through Christ ... ℟ Amen.

Preface: Christ, God and man, the Saviour of all.

The Lord be with you.
℟ And also with you.

Lift up your hearts.
℟ We lift them up to the Lord.

Let us give thanks to the Lord our God.
℟ It is right to give him thanks and praise.

It is truly right and just, our duty and our salvation
always and everywhere to give you thanks, O Lord,
Father most holy, almighty and eternal God:
through Christ our Lord.
It is in him that your promises are fulfilled,
shadows give way to light, the world finds itself
    reborn,
and man is created anew.
By his offering once for all upon the cross,
he wished to gather all your children who were
    dispersed.
Lifted up in glory, he draws all unto himself
as the first-born among many brothers.
And so, Lord, we praise you with all the Angels and
    Saints,
saying in exultation:

Holy, holy, holy Lord ...

Communion Antiphon (Mt 28, 20)

Lo, I am with you always, says the Lord, to the close of the age.
Easter: Alleluia.

Prayer after Communion

Strengthened by heavenly bread, we ask, O Lord,
that by adhering constantly to the Gospel of life
we may become a life-giving leaven and an
    instrument of salvation
for the whole human family.
Through Christ …

℟ Amen.

Solemn Blessing

May the peace of God, which surpasses all
    understanding,
keep your hearts and minds
in the knowledge and love of God, and of his Son,
our Lord Jesus Christ.

℟ Amen.

And may the blessing of almighty God,
the Father, and the Son, + and the Holy Spirit
descend upon you and remain for ever.

℟ Amen.

Mary, Mother of God

Entrance Antiphon (Sedulius)

Hail, holy Mother! The child to whom you gave birth
is the King of heaven and earth for ever.

Opening Prayer

God our Father,
may we always profit by the prayers
of the Virgin Mother Mary,
for you bring us life and salvation
through Jesus Christ her Son,
who lives and reigns with you and the Holy Spirit,
one God, for ever and ever. ℟ Amen.

First Reading
Galatians 4, 4–7 *(see p. 82)*

Responsorial Psalm (Judith 13, 18–20)

℟ You are the highest honour of our race.

May you be blessed, my daughter, by God Most
    High,
beyond all women on earth;
and may the Lord God be blessed,
the creator of heaven and earth. ℟

The trust you have shown
shall not pass from the memories of men,
but shall ever remind them
of the power of God. ℟

God grant you to be always held in honour
and rewarded with blessings,
since you did not consider your own life
when our nation was brought to its knees. ℟

Gospel Acclamation

Alleluia.

Blessed are you, O Virgin Mary, and worthy of all
   praise:

to you was born the Sun of righteousness, Christ
   our God.

Gospel

Luke 2, 4–11 *(see p. 83)*

Intercessions *(see p. 85)*

Prayer over the Gifts

God our Father,
we celebrate at this season
the beginning of our salvation.
On this feast of Mary, the Mother of God,
we ask that our salvation
will be brought to its fulfilment.
We ask this through Christ our Lord. ℟ Amen.

Preface

The Lord be with you.

℟ And also with you.

Lift up your hearts.

℟ We lift them up to the Lord.

Let us give thanks to the Lord our God.

℟ It is right to give him thanks and praise.

Father, all-powerful and ever-living God,
we do well always and everywhere to give you thanks
as we honour the Blessed Virgin Mary.

Through the power of the Holy Spirit,
she became the virgin mother of your only Son,
our Lord Jesus Christ,
who is for ever the light of the world.

Through him the choirs of angels
and all the powers of heaven

praise and worship your glory.
May our voices blend with theirs
as we join in their unending hymn:

Holy, holy, holy ...

Communion Antiphon (from Lk 11, 27)

Blessed is the Virgin Mary, who carried in her womb
the Son of the Eternal Father.

Prayer after Communion

Father,
as we proclaim the Virgin Mary
to be the mother of Christ and the mother of the
    Church,
may our communion with her Son
bring us to salvation.
We ask this through Christ our Lord. ℟ Amen.

APOSTLE SAINT PETER

Entrance Antiphon (Lk 22, 32)

The Lord said to Simon Peter: I have prayed that
your faith may not fail; and you in your turn must
strengthen your brothers.

Opening Prayer

Lord, you gave your apostle Peter the keys of the
    kingdom of heaven,
entrusting him with supreme power to bind and to
    loose.
By the help of his prayers
free us from the bonds of our sins.

We ask this through our Lord Jesus Christ, your Son,
who lives and reigns with you and the Holy Spirit,
one God, for ever and ever.
℟ Amen.

First Reading
1 Peter 2, 4–5.9–10 *(see p. 40)*

Responsorial Psalm
from Colossians 1, 12–14.18–20 *(see p. 41)*

Gospel Acclamation   (Mt 16, 18)
Alleluia.
You are Peter, and on this rock
I will build my church.

Gospel
Matthew 16, 13–19 *(see p. 42)*

Intercessions *(see p. 42)*

Prayer over the Gifts
Lord,
accept our gifts in honour of Peter your apostle,
for by a secret revelation you taught him to
    acknowledge you
as the living God and Christ as your son,
and you gave him the further privilege of
    witnessing to his Lord
by his victorious suffering and death.
We ask this through Christ our Lord.
℟ Amen.

Preface of the Apostles
The Lord be with you.
℟ And also with you.

Lift up your hearts.
℟ We lift them up to the Lord.

Let us give thanks to the Lord our God.
℟ It is right to give him thanks and praise.

Father, all-powerful and ever-living God,
we do well always and everywhere to give you thanks.

You are the eternal Shepherd
who never leaves his flock untended.
Through the apostles
you watch over us and protect us always.
You made them shepherds of the flock
to share in the work of your Son,
and from their place in heaven they guide us still.

And so, with all the choirs of angels in heaven
we proclaim your glory
and join in their unending hymn of praise:

Holy, holy, holy ...

Communion Antiphon (Mt 16, 16–18)

Peter said: You are the Christ, the Son of the living
God.
Jesus answered: You are Peter, the rock on which I
will build my Church.

Prayer after Communion

Lord, hear the prayer of those you have called to
this table of salvation
in honour of Peter your apostle.
Keep us faithful to your Son,
who alone has the word of eternal life,
that he may lead us as the loyal sheep of his flock
to the eternal joys of your kingdom.
We ask this through Christ our Lord.

℟ Amen.

Apostle Saint Paul

Entrance Antiphon (2 Tim 1, 12; 4, 8)

I know whom I have believed. I am sure that he, the just judge, will guard my pledge until the day of judgment.

Opening Prayer

Lord God,
you appointed Paul your apostle to preach the good
   news of salvation.
Fill the entire world with the faith
he carried to so many peoples and nations,
that your Church may continue to grow.
We ask this through our Lord Jesus Christ, your Son,
who lives and reigns with you and the Holy Spirit,
one God, for ever and ever.
℟. Amen.

First Reading

Colossians 1, 24–28 *(see p. 54)*

Responsorial Psalm

from Revelation 15, 3–4 *(see p. 54)*

Gospel Acclamation (Mt 16, 18)

Alleluia.
The Kingdom of God is among you, says the Lord;
take the message of peace to all the world.

Gospel

Matthew 28, 16–20 *(see p. 56)*

Intercessions *(see p. 56)*

Prayer over the Gifts

Lord, as we celebrate this holy eucharist
may your Spirit fill us with the light
which led Paul the apostle
to make your glory known.
We ask this through Christ our Lord. ℟ Amen.

Preface *(see pp. 151–152)*

Communion Antiphon   (Gal 2, 20)

I live by the faith in the Son of God, who loved me
and sacrificed himself for me.

Prayer after Communion

Lord, you renew us with the communion of the body
    and blood of your Son.
May Christ be our life
and nothing separate us from his love.
Following the teachings of Saint Paul, may we live
    in love
for our brothers and sisters.
We ask this through Christ our Lord. ℟ Amen.

FOR THE UNIVERSAL CHURCH

Entrance Antiphon   (cf Eph 1, 9.10)

The Lord has made known to us the mystery of his
will, to unite in Christ all things in heaven and on earth.

Opening Prayer

God our Father,
in your care and wisdom
you extend the kingdom of Christ to embrace the world
to give all men redemption.

The Crossing of the Red Sea, C. Rosselli, Sistine Chapel, Vatican

May the Catholic Church be the sign of our
    salvation,
may it reveal for us the mystery of your love,
and may that love become effective in our lives.

Grant this through our Lord Jesus Christ, your Son,
who lives and reigns with you and the Holy Spirit,
one God, for ever and ever.
℟ Amen.

First Reading

Ephesians 4, 1–7 (see p. 68)

Responsorial Psalm

Psalm 122 (see p. 68)

Gospel Acclamation   (from Jn 4, 8.12)

Alleluia.
God is love: if we remain in love
God remains in us
and his love is made perfect in us.

Gospel

John 17, 20–23 (see p. 69)

Intercessions (see p. 70)

Prayer over the Gifts

God of mercy,
look on our offering,
and by the power of this sacrament
help all who believe in you
to become the holy people you have called to be
    your own.
We ask this in the name of Jesus the Lord. ℟ Amen

Preface

The Lord be with you.
℟ And also with you.

Lift up your hearts.
℟ We lift them up to the Lord.

Let us give thanks to the Lord our God.
℟ It is right to give him thanks and praise.

Father, all-powerful and ever-living God,
we do well always and everywhere to give you thanks.
When your children sinned
and wandered far from your friendship,
you reunited them with yourself
through the blood of your Son
and the power of the Holy Spirit.
You gather them into your Church,
to be one as you, Father, are one
with your Son and the Holy Spirit.
You call them to be your people,
to praise your wisdom in all your works.
You make them the body of Christ
and the dwelling-place of the Holy Spirit.
In our joy we sing to your glory
with all the choirs of angels:
Holy, holy, holy ...

Communion Antiphon   (Rev 22, 17.20)

The Spirit and the bride say: Come.
Amen, come, Lord Jesus.

Prayer after Communion

God our Father, we are sustained by your sacraments;
we are renewed by this pledge of love at your altar.
May we live by the promises of your love which we
    receive,
and become a leaven in the world
to bring salvation to mankind.
Grant this through Christ our Lord. ℟ Amen.

The Church, Body of Christ and living temple of the Spirit
Pentecost, El Greco, Prado Museum, Madrid

The Sacrament
of Penance

Reconciliation through the Sacrament of Penance is not only an essential part of the pilgrims' sign of conversion but might be described as the introduction to all the Jubilee practices.

The Church, having received from Christ the power to forgive sin in his name (cf. Mt 16, 19; Jn 20, 23), is in the world the living presence of God's love, who opens his merciful arms to embrace human weakness.

The Sacrament of Penance opens the way to the conversion of the sinner and the restoration of the grace of justification obtained through Christ's sacrifice. By the confession of sin, the believer truly receives forgiveness and shares again in the Eucharist thus manifesting communion with the Father and with the Church. (IM 9)

"The sacrament of Penance is a whole consisting in three actions of the penitent and the priest's absolution. The penitent's acts are repentance, confession or disclosure of sins to the priest, and the intention to make reparation and do works of reparation." (CCC 1491)

"One who desires to obtain reconciliation with God and with the Church, must confess to a priest all the unconfessed grave sins he remembers after having carefully examined his conscience. The confession of venial faults, without being necessary in itself, is nevertheless strongly recommended by the Church." (CCC 1493)

"Individual and integral confession of grave sins followed by absolution remains the only ordinary means of reconciliation with God and with the Church." (CCC 1497)

Examination of Conscience

Following the example of the prodigal son, who "came to himself", examine your conscience by the light of the Gospel and find out when you behaved contrary to the teaching of our Lord Jesus Christ in thoughts, words and deeds.

Before God

Is my heart set on God, so that I really love him above all things?

Do I take part regularly in Mass on Sundays and Feasts?

Do I begin and end my day with prayer?

Have I love and reverence for the name of God, the Blessed Virgin Mary and Saints?

Am I ashamed to witness to my faith in God in my daily life?

Am I making an effort to grow spiritually? How? When?

Have I failed to keep my baptismal commitment?

Do I rebel against taking up the Cross which God sends?

Do I turn to God only when I am in need?

Relationship with neighbours

Have I a genuine love for my neighbours? Am I well-disposed, able to forgive offences?

Do I judge without mercy in thoughts and words?

Do I speak ill, slander, steal?

Am I intolerant, envious, hot-tempered?

Do I take care of the poor, the sick, defenceless people?

Am I sincere and honest in my dealings with others?

Have I been the cause of another's committing sin?

In my family life, have I contributed to the well-being and happiness of the rest of the family by patience and genuine love?

Do I exercise responsible parenthood?

Do I care for and respect the environment in which I live?

Self-examination

Do I truly live as a Christian and give a good
    example to others?
Do I go to excess in matters of food and drink?
Am I too concerned about myself, my health, my
    success?
Do I use leisure time properly? Am I lazy?
Have I participated in things which offend both
    Christian and human decency?
Have I kept my senses and my whole body pure and
    chaste as a temple of the Holy Spirit?
Do I bear grudges; do I contemplate revenge?
Do I share my possessions with the less fortunate?
Am I always ready to take offence and act
    impatiently?
Do I seek to be humble and bring peace?

RITE OF PENANCE

In the name of the Father and Son and Holy Spirit.
℟ Amen.

The Priest addresses the penitent with these or similar words:
May the Lord enlighten your heart with faith, and
give you a true knowledge of your sins and trust in
his mercy. ℟ Amen.

*The priest may read a short Scripture passage, then the
penitent makes his or her confession. The priest counsels
the penitent and gives a penance, usually some prayers or
a charitable work. The penitent accepts the penance and
shows sorrow for sin by saying an* Act of Contrition*:*

O my God, I am very sorry that I have sinned
    against you,
because you are so good,
and by the help of your holy grace, I will not sin again.

Remember your mercy, Lord,
and the love you have shown from of old.
Do not remember the sins of my youth;
in your love remember me. (Ps 24, 6–7)

Have mercy on me, God, in your kindness;
in your compassion blot out my offence.
My offences truly I know them;
my sin is always before me.
Against you, you alone, have I sinned.
A pure heart create for me, O God;
put a steadfast spirit within me.
Do not cast me away from your presence
and deprive me of your holy spirit.
Give me again the joy of your help;
with a spirit of fervour sustain me,
O rescue me, God, my helper. (from Ps 51)

Lord Jesus, Son of God,
have mercy on me a sinner.

The priest then gives absolution saying:

God the Father of mercies, through the death and
resurrection of his Son, has reconciled the world to
himself and sent the Holy Spirit among us for the
forgiveness of sins; through the ministry of the
Church may God give you pardon and peace, and I
absolve you from your sins in the name of the Father,
and of the Son, and of the Holy Spirit. ℟ Amen.

Give thanks to the Lord, for He is good.
℟ His mercy endures for ever.

*The penitent is then dismissed by the priest in the peace
of Christ.*

Penitential Celebrations

A community penitential celebration is proposed for use in a Basilica or in another Church, even if the individual confession takes place at another moment.

Opening Rites

After a hymn the priest greets the people, saying:

Grace and peace be with you
from God the Father
and from Jesus Christ
who loved us
and washed away our sins in his blood.

℟ And also with you.

Then the priest or another minister speaks briefly about the purpose of the celebration and invites all to pray, using these or similar words:

Brothers and sisters, God calls us to conversion; let us therefore ask him for the grace of sincere repentance.

After a brief period of silence the priest sings or says the prayer:

Almighty and merciful God, you have brought us together in the name of your Son to receive your mercy and grace in our time of need. Open our eyes to see the evil we have done. Touch our hearts and convert us to yourself.

Where sin has divided and scattered, may your love make one again; where sin has brought weakness, may your power heal and strengthen; where sin has brought death, may your spirit raise to new life.

Give us a new heart to love you, so that our lives may reflect the image of your Son. May the world see the glory of Christ revealed in your Church, and come to know that he is the one whom you have sent, Jesus Christ, your Son, our Lord. ℟ Amen.

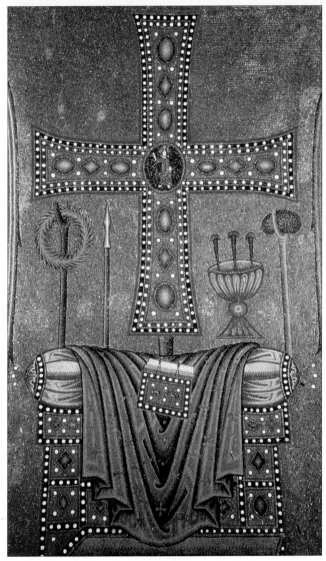

*Gall and vinegar, a reed and a spear, nails and thorns. They
pierced with a lance the body from which flowed blood and water*
(Venantius Fortunatus, *Pange lingua*)
THE "THRONE PREPARED" FOR THE SECOND COMING OF CHRIST,
Saint Paul outside the Walls, Rome

165

THE WORD OF GOD

From the Letter of Saint Paul to the Ephesians (4, 23–32)

Brothers and sisters, your mind must be renewed by a spiritual revolution so that you can put on the new self that has been created in God's way, in the goodness and holiness of the truth. So from now on, there must be no more lies: you must speak the truth to one another, since we are all parts of one another. Even if you are angry, you must not sin: never let the sun set on your anger or else you will give the devil a foothold. Anyone who was a thief must stop stealing; he should try to find some useful manual work instead, and be able to do some good by helping others that are in need. Guard against foul talk; let your words be for the improvement of others, as occasion offers, and do good to your listeners, otherwise you will only be grieving the Holy Spirit of God who has marked you with his seal for you to be set free when the day comes. Never have grudges against others, or lose your temper, or raise your voice to anybody, or call each other names, or allow any sort of spitefulness. Be friends with one another, and kind, forgiving each other as readily as God forgave you in Christ.

℟ Create in me, O God, a new heart. (from Ps 51)

Have mercy on me, God, in your kindness.*
In your compassion blot out my offence. ℟
O wash me more and more from my guilt*
and cleanse me from my sin. ℟
Make me hear rejoicing and gladness,*
that the bones you have crushed may revive. ℟
From my sins turn away your face*
and blot out all my guilt. ℟
A pure heart create for me, O God,*
put a steadfast spirit within me. ℟
Do not cast me away from your presence,*
nor deprive me of your holy spirit. ℟

Give me again the joy of your help;*
with a spirit of fervour sustain me. ℟

From the Gospel according to Matthew   (5, 1–12)

Seeing the crowds, he went up the hill. There he sat down and was joined by his disciples. Then he began to speak. This is what he taught them:
"How happy are the poor in spirit;
theirs is the kingdom of heaven.
Happy the gentle:
they shall have the earth for their heritage.
Happy those who mourn:
they shall be comforted.
Happy those who hunger and thirst for what is right:
they shall be satisfied.
Happy the merciful:
they shall have mercy shown them.
Happy the pure in heart: they shall see God.
Happy the peacemakers:
they shall be called sons of God.
Happy those who are persecuted in the cause of the right:
theirs is the kingdom of heaven.
"Happy are you when people abuse you and persecute you and speak all kinds of calumny against you on my account. Rejoice and be glad, for your reward will be great in heaven; this is how they persecuted the prophets before you."

There follows a homily on the readings, related to the Examination of Conscience.

ACT OF PENITENCE

I confess to almighty God, and to you, my brothers and sisters, that I have sinned through my own fault
in my thoughts and in my words,
in what I have done, and in what I have failed to do;
and I ask blessed Mary, ever virgin, all the angels and saints,
and you, my brothers and sisters,
to pray for me to the Lord our God.

*I will arise and go to my father, and I will say to him, "Father,
I have sinned against you". But the father said: "Let us make a
feast"* (Lk 15, 18. 22) THE RETURN OF THE PRODIGAL SON,
Ugolino da Belluno, Shrine of San Gabriele, Gran Sasso

The priest may sprinkle those present with blessed water and say:

Purge me with hyssop and I shall be clean,
wash me and I shall be whiter than snow.

PRAYER TOGETHER

Stand.

Christ our Saviour is our advocate with the Father:
with humble hearts let us ask him to forgive us our sins
and cleanse us from every stain:

You were sent with good news for the poor and
    healing for the contrite.

℟ Lord, have mercy.

You came to call sinners, not the just. ℟
You forgave the many sins of the woman who
    showed you great love. ℟
You did not shun the company of outcasts and
    sinners. ℟
You carried back to the fold the sheep that had
    strayed. ℟
You did not condemn the woman taken in adultery,
    but sent her away in peace. ℟
You called Zacchaeus to repentance and a new life. ℟
You promised Paradise to the repentant thief. ℟
You are always interceding for us at the right hand
    of the Father. ℟

Now, in obedience to Christ himself, let us join in
prayer to the Father, asking him to forgive us as we
forgive others:

Our Father.

Father, our source of life,
you know our weakness.
May we reach out with joy to grasp your hand
and walk more readily in your ways.
We ask this through Christ our Lord.   ℟ Amen.

A Marian devotion may end this act of prayer (p. 235).

Morning and Evening Prayer

The Liturgy of the Hours, Morning and Evening Prayer, composed of hymns, psalms, canticles and readings from Scripture, "is truly the voice of the bride addressed to her bridegroom; it is the very prayer which Christ Himself, together with His body, addresses to the Father."

(Sacrosanctum Concilium, n. 84)

Two sets of texts are given, one for Sundays and the other for weekdays.

Introduction

O God, come to my aid.
O Lord, make haste to help me.

Glory be to the Father and to the Son and to the Holy Spirit, as it was in the beginning, is now, and ever shall be, world without end.
Amen. Alleluia (the Alleluia is omitted in Lent).

A suitable hymn may be inserted at this point.

Conclusion

The Lord be with you.
℟ And also with you.

May Almighty God bless you, the Father and the Son, + and the Holy Spirit.
℟ Amen.

Go in peace.
℟ Thanks be to God.

If the one who presides is not an ordained minister, the Office ends:

May the Lord bless us and keep us from all harm; and may he lead us to eternal life.
℟ Amen.

Gospel Canticles

Canticle of Zechariah (Lk 1, 68-79)

Blessed be the Lord, the God of Israel;*
    he has visited his people and redeemed them.

He has raised up for us a mighty saviour,*
    in the house of David, his servant;

as he promised by the lips of holy men,*
    those who were his prophets from of old.

A saviour who would free us from our foes,*
    from the hands of all who hate us.

So his love for our fathers is fulfilled*
    and his holy covenant remembered.

He swore to Abraham our father to grant us:*
    that free from fear, and saved from the hands of
    our foes,

we might serve him in holiness and justice*
    all the days of our life in his presence.

As for you, little child,*
    you shall be called the prophet of the Most High;

you shall go ahead of the Lord *
    to prepare his ways before him,

to make known to his people their salvation*
    through forgiveness of all their sins.

The loving-kindness of the heart of our God*
    who visits us like the dawn from on high.

He will give light to those in darkness,
    those who dwell in the shadow of death,*
    and guide us into the way of peace.

Glory.

Canticle of Mary

My soul glorifies the Lord,*
  my spirit rejoices in God, my Saviour

He looks on his servant in her lowliness;*
  henceforth all ages will call me blessed.

The Almighty works marvels for me.*
  Holy is his Name.

His mercy is from age to age,*
  on those who fear him.

He puts forth his arm in strength,*
  and scatters the proud-hearted.

He casts the mighty from their thrones,*
  and raises the lowly.

He fills the starving with good things,*
  and the rich he has sent away empty.

He protects Israel, his servant,*
  remembering his mercy,

the mercy promised to our fathers,*
  to Abraham and his sons for ever.

Glory. *(Latin text p. 245)*

Morning Prayer

Introduction *(see p. 170).*

Hymn

On this day, the first of days,
God the Father's name we praise
who creation's Lord and spring
did the world from darkness bring.

On this day th'eternal Son
over death his triumph won;
on this day the Spirit came
with the gifts of living flame.

On this day his people raise
one pure sacrifice of praise,
and with all the saints above,
tell of Christ's redeeming love.

Praise, O God, to you be given,
praise on earth and praise in heaven,
praise to the eternal Son,
who this day our victory won.

Or:

God whose almighty Word
chaos and darkness heard,
and took their flight;
hear us, we humbly pray,
and where the Gospel-day
sheds not its glorious ray
let there be light.

Saviour, who came to bring
on your redeeming wing
healing and sight,

health to the sick in mind,
sight to the inly blind,
ah! now to all mankind
let there be light.

Spirit of truth and love,
life-giving, holy dove,
speed forth your flight!
Move on the water's face,
bearing the lamp of grace,
and in earth's darkest place
let there be light!

Ant. 1 From the dawn I long for you O God:
that I may see your glory and power (alleluia).

Psalm 63

O God, you are my God, for you I long;*
for you my soul is thirsting.
My body pines for you*
like a dry, weary land without water.
So I gaze on you in the sanctuary*
to see your strength and your glory.
For your love is better than life;*
my lips will speak your praise.
So I will bless you all my life;*
in your name I will lift up my hands.
My soul shall be filled as with a banquet;*
my mouth shall praise you with joy.
On my bed I remember you;*
on you I muse through the night.
For you have been my help;*
in the shadow of your wings I rejoice.
My soul clings to you;*
your right hand holds me fast.

Glory.   Ant. 1

Ant. 2 In the midst of the fire, the three young men sang
with one voice: Blessed be God (alleluia).

THE THREE YOUNG MEN IN THE FIERY FURNACE, Catacombs of Priscilla, Rome

Canticle Daniel 3, 57–88.56

O all you works of the Lord, O bless the Lord.*
  To him be highest glory and praise for ever.
And you, angels of the Lord, O bless the Lord.*
  To him be highest glory and praise for ever.

And you, the heavens of the Lord, O bless the Lord.*
  And you, clouds of the sky, O bless the Lord.
And you, all armies of the Lord, O bless the Lord.*
  To him be highest glory and praise for ever.

And you, sun and moon, O bless the Lord.*
  And you, the stars of the heav'ns, O bless
  the Lord.
And you, showers and rain, O bless the Lord.*
  To him be highest glory and praise for ever.

And you, all you breezes and winds, O bless
  the Lord.*
  And you, fire and heat, O bless the Lord.

And you, cold and heat, O bless the Lord.*
  To him be highest glory and praise for ever.

And you, showers and dew, O bless the Lord.*
  And you, frosts and cold, O bless the Lord.
And you, frost and snow, O bless the Lord.*
  To him be highest glory and praise for ever.

And you, night-time and day, O bless the Lord.*
  And you, darkness and light, O bless the Lord.
And you, lightning and clouds, O bless the Lord.*
  To him be highest glory and praise for ever.

O let the earth bless the Lord.*
  To him be highest glory and praise for ever.

And you, mountains and hills, O bless the Lord.*
  And you, all plants of the earth, O bless the Lord.
And you, fountains and springs, O bless the Lord.*
  To him be highest glory and praise for ever.

And, rivers and seas, O bless the Lord.*
  And you, creatures of the sea, O bless the Lord.
And you, every bird in the sky, O bless the Lord.
  And you, wild beasts and tame, O bless the Lord.*
To him be highest glory and praise for ever.

And you, children of men, O bless the Lord.*
  To him be highest glory and praise for ever.

O Israel, bless the Lord. O bless the Lord.*
  And you, priests of the Lord, O bless the Lord.
And you, servants of the Lord, O bless the Lord.*
  To him be highest glory and praise for ever.

And you, spirits and souls of the just, O bless the
  Lord.*
  And you, holy and humble of heart, O bless the Lord.
Ananias, Azarias, Mizael, O bless the Lord.*
  To him be highest glory and praise for ever.

Let us praise the Father, the Son and Holy Spirit;*
   To you be highest glory and praise for ever.
May you be blessed, O Lord, in the heavens,*
   To you be highest glory and praise for ever.

There is no Gloria.

Ant. 2

Ant. 3 The children of the Church rejoice in their King
(alleluia)

Psalm 149

Sing a new song to the Lord,*
his praise in the assembly of the faithful.
Let Israel rejoice in its Maker;*
let Zion's sons exult in their king.
Let them praise his name with dancing*
and make music with timbrel and harp,
for the Lord takes delight in his people;*
he crowns the poor with salvation.
Let the faithful rejoice in their glory,*
shout for joy and take their rest.
Let the praise of God be on their lips*
and a two-edged sword in their hands
to deal out vengeance to the nations*
and punishment on all the peoples,
to bind their kings in chains*
and their nobles in fetters of iron,
to carry out the sentence pre-ordained*
this honour is for all his faithful.

Glory. Ant. 3

Short Reading   Revelation 7, 10. 12

Victory to our God, who sits on the throne, and to
the Lamb! Praise and glory and wisdom and
thanksgiving and honour and power and strength to
our God for ever and ever. Amen.

Short Responsory

℟. You are the Christ, the Son of the living God. Have mercy on us. *(Repeat)*
℣. You are seated at the right hand of the Father. ℟.
Glory be. ℟.

Canticle *(see p. 171).*

Intercessions
Let us pray to Christ the Lord, the sun who enlightens all men, whose light will never fail us:

℟. Lord, our Saviour, give us life.

Lord of the sun and the stars, we thank you for the gift of a new day; and we celebrate the day of resurrection. ℟.

Bring us to share with joy this Sunday's eucharist; nourish us by your word, and by your body. ℟.

Lord, grant us your gifts, though we are unworthy; with all our hearts we thank you. ℟.

Guide and protect Pope (N.); uphold him with your wisdom and guide him today and always. ℟.

Our Father.

The Prayer is that of the Sunday.

Or:

O God, who has given us the Saviour and the Holy Spirit, look with favour on your children by adoption, that all who believe in Christ may be given true freedom and eternal inheritance.
Through our Lord Jesus Christ.

Conclusion *(see p.170).*

Evening Prayer – Vespers

Introduction *(see p. 170).*

Hymn

O Trinity of blessed light,
O unity of primal night,
As now the fiery sun departs,
So shed your radiance in our hearts.

To you our morning song of praise,
To you our evening prayer we raise:
May we behold your glorious face,
And joy in your eternal grace.

CIRCLE OF CREATION, Narthex of St Mark's, Venice

Ant. 1 The Lord will extend his rule over Zion,
and will rule for ever (alleluia).

Psalm 110, 1–5.7

The Lord's revelation to my Master:
"Sit on my right:*
your foes I will put beneath your feet."
The Lord will wield from Zion
your sceptre of power;*
rule in the midst of all your foes.
"A prince from the day of your birth
on the holy mountains;*
from the womb before the dawn I begot you."
The Lord has sworn an oath he will not change
"You are a priest for ever,*
a priest like Melchizedek of old."
The Master standing at your right hand*
will shatter kings in the day of his wrath.
He shall drink from the stream by the wayside,*
and therefore he shall lift up his head.

Glory. Ant. 1

Ant. 2 Tremble, O earth, before the Lord,
in the presence of the God of Jacob.

Psalm 114

When Israel came forth from Egypt,*
Jacob's sons from an alien people,
Judah became the Lord's temple,*
Israel became his kingdom.

The sea fled at the sight;*
the Jordan turned back on its course;
the mountains leapt like rams*
and the hills like yearling sheep.

Why was it, sea, that you fled,*
that you turned back, Jordan, on your course;
mountains, that you leapt like rams,*
hills, like yearling sheep?

Tremble, O earth, before the Lord,*
in the presence of the God of Jacob,
who turns the rock into a pool*
and flint into a spring of water.

Glory. Ant. 2

(In Lent see p.182)

Ant. 3 The Lord reigns: to him be glory, alleluia, alleluia.

Canticle from Revelation 19, 1–7

Alleluia.
Salvation and glory and power belong to our God,*
His judgments are true and just.

Alleluia.
Praise our God, all you his servants,*
You who fear him, small and great.

Alleluia.
The Lord our God, the almighty, reigns.*
Let us rejoice and exult and give him the glory.

Alleluia.
The Marriage of the Lamb has come.*
And his bride has made herself ready.

Glory.

Ant. 3 The Lord reigns: to him be glory, alleluia, alleluia.

Ant. 3 (in Lent) We adore you, O Christ, and we bless you, because by your cross you have redeemed the world.

Canticle   from 1 Peter 2, 21–24

Christ suffered for you leaving you an example*
that you should follow in his steps.

He committed no sin;*
no guile was found on his lips.

When he was reviled,*
he did not revile in return.

When he suffered, he did not threaten;*
but he trusted to him who judges justly.

He himself bore our sins in his body on the tree,*
that we might die to sin and live to righteousness.

By his wounds you have been healed.

Glory. Ant. 3

Short Reading   2 Corinthians 1, 3-4

Blessed be the God and Father of our Lord Jesus Christ, a gentle father and the God of all consolation, who comforts us in all our sorrows, so that we can offer others, in their sorrows, the consolation that we have received from God ourselves.

Short Responsory

℟ Blessed are you, Lord, in the highest. *(Repeat)*
℣ To you be praise and glory for ever,
In the highest heavens.

Glory to the Father and to the Son and to the Holy Spirit.
Blessed are you, Lord, in the highest heavens.

Ant. to the Magnificat.
To him who was, and is, and is to come,
be honour and power for ever and ever (alleluia).

Magnificat *(see p. 172).*

Intercessions

Christ is our head and we are the members. To him be praise and glory for ever. Let us praise him:

℟ Your kingdom come, O Lord.

May your Church, Lord, be a living sacrament and means of unity for the human race. ℟

Help the college of bishops in union with our Pope N. Pour into them your Spirit of unity, of love and peace. ℟

May all Christians be united with you, head of the Church, and give true witness to your Gospel. ℟

Give peace to the world, and grant that a new order of justice, brotherhood and sisterhood may be created. ℟

Give our departed brothers and sisters the glory of resurrection, and make us share in their blessedness. ℟

Our Father.

The Prayer is that of the Sunday *(or see p. 178).*

Conclusion *(see p. 170).*

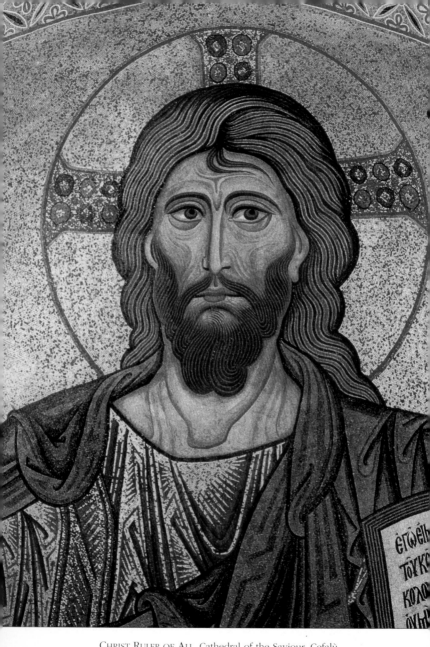

CHRIST RULER OF ALL, Cathedral of the Saviour, Cefalù

Morning Prayer – Lauds

Introduction *(see p.170).*

Hymn

> The Father's glory, Christ our light,
> With love and mercy comes to bless
> Our fallen world, and be the way
> That leads from sin to holiness.
>
> Christ yesterday and Christ today,
> For all eternity the same,
> the image of our hidden God:
> Eternal wisdom is his name.
>
> He keeps his work from age to age,
> Is with us to the end of days;
> A cloud by day, a flame by night,
> To go before us on his ways.
>
> We bless you, Father, fount of light,
> And Christ, your well-beloved Son,
> Who with the Spirit dwell in us:
> Immortal Trinity in One.

Ant. 1 Let all who are thirsty come; all who want it may have the water of life.

Psalm 42

Like the deer that yearns* for running streams,
　　so my soul is yearning* for you my God.
My soul is thirsting for God,* the God of my life:
　　when can I enter and see* the face of God?
My tears have become my bread,* by night, by day,
　　as I hear it said all the day long* "Where is your God?"

These things will I remember*
   as I pour out my soul;
how I would lead the rejoicing crowd*
   into the house of God,
amid cries of gladness and thanksgiving,*
   the throng wild with joy.
Why are you cast down, my soul;*
   why groan within me?
Hope in God; I will praise him still,*
   my saviour and my God.
My soul is cast down within me*
   as I think of you,
from the country of Jordan and Mount Hermon,*
   from the Hill of Mizar.
Deep is calling on deep,*
   in the roar of waters;
your torrents and all your waves*
   swept over me.
By day the Lord will send*
   his loving kindness;
by night I will sing to him,*
   praise the God of my life.
I will say to God, my rock:*
   Why have you forgotten me?
Why do I go mourning,*
   oppressed by the foe?
With cries that pierce me to the heart,*
   my enemies revile me,
saying to me all the day long:*
   Where is your God?
Why are you cast down, my soul;*
   why groan within me?
Hope in God; I will praise him still,*
   my saviour and my God.

Glory. Ant. 1

Ant. 2 Show us, Lord, the light of your mercy.

Canticle   Sirach 36, 1–5.10–13

Save us, God of all things,*
strike all the nations with terror;
raise your hand against foreign nations,*
that they may see the greatness of your might.
Our sufferings proved your holiness to them;*
let their downfall prove your glory to us.
Let them know, as we ourselves know,*
that there is no other God but you.
Give us signs again, work further wonders,*
clothe your hand, your right arm in glory.
Assemble all the tribes of Jacob,*
as when they first received their inheritance.
Pity the poor people called by your name,*
pity Israel, chosen as you first-born.
Have compassion on the holy city,*
Jerusalem, the place of your rest.
Let Zion ring with your praises,*
let your temple be filled with your glory.

Glory. Ant. 2

Psalm 19, 2–7

The heavens proclaim the glory of God,*
and the firmament shows forth the work of his
    hands.
Day unto day takes up the story,*
and night unto night makes known the message.

No speech, no word, no voice is heard,
yet their span extends through all the earth,*
their words to the utmost bounds of the world.
There he has placed a tent for the sun;
it comes forth like a bridegroom coming from his
    tent,*
rejoices like a champion to run its course.

At the end of the sky is the rising of the sun;
to the furthest end of the sky is its course.*
There is nothing concealed from its burning heat.

Glory.

Ant. 3 Blessed are you, Lord, in the heights of
heaven.

Short Reading   Zephaniah 3, 14–18

Shout for joy, daughter of Zion, Israel, shout aloud!
Rejoice, exult with all your heart, daughter of
Jerusalem! Yahweh has repealed your sentence; he
has driven your enemies away. The Lord, the King of
Israel, is in your midst; you have no more evil to fear.
When that day comes, word will come to Jerusalem:
Zion, have no fear, do not let your hands fall limp!
Yahweh your God is in your midst, a victorious
warrior. He will exult with joy over you, he will
renew you by his love; he will dance with shouts of
joy for you as on a day of festival.

Short Responsory

℟ Rejoice in the Lord, O you just; for praise is fitting
for loyal hearts. *(Repeat)*

℣ Sing to him a new song.

℟ Rejoice in the Lord, O you just; for praise is fitting
for loyal hearts.
Glory . . .

℟ Rejoice in the Lord, O you just; for praise is fitting
for loyal hearts.

Antiphon for Benedictus: Blessed be the Lord, for he
has visited us and freed us.

Benedictus *(see page 171).*

Intercessions

Christ has given us all a share in his priesthood. We offer our prayers and ourselves in union with him.
℟ Lord, accept our love and service.

Jesus Christ, you are the eternal priest: make this morning's offering acceptable to the Father. ℟

Lord, you are love itself: grant that we may love you. ℟

Guide and protect with your Spirit the Pope (N.) who has the task of presiding over your Church; may he be for your people the visible foundation of unity in faith. ℟

Give us today the fruits of the Holy Spirit: make us patient, kind and gentle. ℟

Give us the discernment to know the needs of our neighbours, and give us the courage to love them as brothers. ℟

Our Father.

The Prayer
See the texts for the respective basilicas. Or:

O God, our salvation, who has made us children of light, guide us on our journey, that we may become workers for truth and witnesses to the Gospel. Through our Lord Jesus Christ.

Conclusion *(see p. 170).*

Eve, the mother of all living, before God her creator
FRESCO, Sistine Chapel, Vatican, Michelangelo

Evening Prayer – Vespers

Introduction *(see p. 170)*.

Hymn

O blest creator, God most high,
Great ruler of the star-filled sky,
You clothe the day with radiant light,
In shadows dark enfold the night.

We thank you for this day now gone;
And pray you, as the night draws on,
Help us, your children, thus to raise
Our evening offering of praise.

To you our hearts their music bring,
To you our gathered voices sing;
To you our hearts' deep longings soar,
And you our chastened souls adore.

O Christ the Father's only Son,
And Spirit of them both, but One;
God over all, whom all obey,
Shield us, great Trinity, we pray.

Ant. 1 The Lord is my light and my help;
whom shall I fear?

Psalm 27, 1-6

The Lord is my light and my help;*
whom shall I fear?
The Lord is the stronghold of my life;*
before whom shall I shrink?

When evil-doers draw near*
to devour my flesh,
it is they, my enemies and foes,*
who stumble and fall.

Though an army encamp against me,*
    my heart would not fear.
Though war break out against me,*
    even then would I trust.

There is one thing I ask of the Lord,*
    for this I long:
to live in the house of the Lord*
    all the days of my life,
to savour the sweetness of the Lord,*
    to behold his temple.

For there he keeps me safe in his tent;*
    in the day of evil;
He hides me in the shelter of his tent*
    on a rock he sets me safe.

And now my head shall be raised*
    above my foes who surround me,
and I shall offer within his tent
    a sacrifice of joy.*
I will sing and make music for the Lord.

Glory. Ant. 1

Ant. 2 It is your face, O Lord, that I seek;
    hide not your face.

Psalm 27, 7–14

O Lord, hear my voice when I call;*
    have mercy and answer.
Of you my heart has spoken:*
    Seek his face.

It is your face, O Lord, that I seek;*
    hide not your face.
Dismiss not your servant in anger;*
    you have been my help.

Do not abandon or forsake me,*
    O God my help!

Though father and mother forsake me,*
   the Lord will receive me.

Instruct me, Lord, in your way;*
   on an even path lead me.
When they lie in ambush protect me*
   from my enemy's greed.
False witnesses rise against me,*
   breathing out fury.

I am sure I shall see the Lord's goodness*
   in the land of the living.
Hope in him, hold firm and take heart!*
   Hope in the Lord!

Glory.

Ant. 2 It is your face, O Lord, that I seek;
   hide not your face.

Ant. 3 He is the firstborn of all creation;
   he is supreme over all creatures.

Canticle   (from Col. 1, 3.12–20)

Let us give thanks to the Father,
who has qualified us to share*
in the inheritance of the saints in light.
He has delivered us from the dominion of darkness*
and transferred us to the kingdom of his beloved Son,
in whom we have redemption,*
the forgiveness of sins.
He is the image of the invisible God,*
the firstborn of all creation,
for in him all things were created, in heaven and on
   earth,*
visible and invisible.
All things were created*
through him and for him.
He is before all things,*
and in him all things hold together.

He is the head of the body, the Church;*
he is the beginning,
the firstborn from the dead,*
that in everything he might be pre-eminent.

For in him all the fullness of God was pleased to
    dwell,*
and through him to reconcile to himself all things,
whether on earth or in heaven,*
making peace by the blood of his cross.

Glory. Ant. 3

Short Reading   James 1, 22. 25

You must do what the word tells you, and not just
listen to it and deceive yourselves. But the man who
looks steadily at the perfect law of freedom and
makes that his habit, not listening and then
forgetting, but actively putting it into practice, will be
happy in all that he does.

Short Responsory

℟ Redeem me, Lord, and show me your mercy.
  (Repeat)

℣ Do not cast me away with sinners. ℟

Glory . . .

Magnificat Ant. The Almighty has done great things
for me; holy is his name.

Magnificat *(see page 172).*

Intercessions

The world is ablaze with the glory of God, who cares
for his chosen people with infinite love. In the name
of the Church we pray:

℟ Lord, show your love to all men.

Be mindful of your Church: keep her free from evil and make her perfect in your love. ℟

Let all peoples acknowledge that you alone are God, and that Jesus Christ is your Son; give them the light of faith. ℟

Grant to those around us all that they need, so that they may show thankfulness and live in peace. ℟

Keep us mindful of those whose work is hard and unrewarding: may we give every man the respect which is his right. ℟

Give peace to those who have died today; grant them eternal rest. ℟

Our Father.

Prayer
See the prayers given for the relevant Basilicas.

Or:

Lord, support us as we pray, protect us day and night, so that we who live in a world of change may always draw strength from you, with whom there is no shadow of alteration.
Through our Lord Jesus Christ.

Conclusion *(see p. 170).*

THE MYSTERY OF FAITH, Raphael, Vatican

196

Adoration of the Blessed Sacrament

For purpose of meditation and reflection during exposition of the Blessed Sacrament the following texts from Scripture are given. You are invited: 1. to deepen your understanding of the words of Jesus on the mystery of the Bread of eternal life, and so give thanks to the Father for the wonderful sacrament of the Eucharist; 2. to keep in mind that we, like the disciples on the road to Emmaus, need time to deepen our understanding of the presence of Christ in the Eucharist.

A GOSPEL MEDITATION

1.

Listen to the Word of the Lord from the Gospel according to John   (6, 27–35)

Jesus said, "Do not labour for the food which perishes, but for the food which endures to eternal life, which the Son of man will give to you; for on him has God the Father set his seal." Then they said to him, "What must we do, to be doing the works of God?" Jesus answered them, "This is the work of God, that you believe in him whom he has sent." So they said to him, "Then what sign do you do, that we may see, and believe you? What work do you perform? Our fathers ate the manna in the wilderness; as it is written, 'He gave them bread from heaven to eat.'" Jesus then said to them, "Truly, truly, I say to you, it was not Moses who gave you the bread from heaven; my Father gives you the true bread from heaven. For the bread of God is that which comes down from heaven, and gives life to the world." They said to him, "Lord, give us this bread always." Jesus said to them, "I am the bread of life; he who comes to me shall not hunger, and he who believes in me shall never thirst."

After a moment of silence, a suitable hymn or sacred song can be sung. A period of personal prayer *follows. A second passage from the Gospel is read:*

Listen to the Word of the Lord from the Gospel according to John   (6, 53–58)

Jesus said to them, "Truly, truly, I say to you, unless you eat the flesh of the Son of man and drink his blood, you have no life in you; he who eats my flesh and drinks my blood has eternal life, and I will raise him up at the last day. For my flesh is food indeed, and my blood is drink indeed. He who eats my flesh and drinks my blood abides in me, and I in him. As the living Father sent me, and I live because of the Father, so he who eats me will live because of me. This is the bread which came down from heaven, not such as the fathers ate and died; he who eats this bread will live for ever."

2.

Listen to the Word of the Lord from the Gospel according to Luke   (24, 13–35)

See p. 120: the passage may be divided into two parts, divided by a silent pause.

ADORATION

After the meditation there follows a period of prolonged silent adoration which is concluded by the following acclamations and supplications to Christ:

Body of Christ conceived of the Blessed Virgin Mary:
℟ To you be praise and glory for ever.

Body of Christ, sacrificed on the cross:
℟ To you be praise and glory for ever.

Body of Christ, risen from the tomb:
℟ To you be praise and glory for ever.

Blood of Christ, price of our ransom:
℟ To you be praise and glory for ever.

Blood of Christ, the seal of new alliance:
℟ To you be praise and glory for ever.

Blood of Christ, drink of eternal life:
℟ To you be praise and glory for ever.

Heart of Christ, pierced through with the lance:
℟ To you be praise and glory for ever.

Heart of Christ, rich in mercy:
℟ To you be praise and glory for ever.

Heart of Christ, source of love:
℟ To you be praise and glory for ever.

Living bread come down the heaven:
℟ Give us your salvation.

Living word of the Father:
℟ Give us your salvation.

Giver of the Holy Spirit:
℟ Give us your salvation.

Bridegroom of Holy Church:
℟ Give us your salvation.

Redeemer of the world:
℟ Give us your salvation.

Friend of the young and the poor:
℟ Give us your salvation.

When you come on the last day:
℟ Give us your salvation.

Prayer

Lord Jesus Christ, you gave us the Eucharist as the memorial of your suffering and death. May our worship of this sacrament of your body and blood help us to experience the salvation you won for us and the peace of the kingdom where you live with the Father and the Holy Spirit, one God, for ever and ever. ℟ Amen.

The Way of the Cross

The custom of pausing in prayer at the places associated with the Passion of Jesus was much loved by pilgrims to Jerusalem. Those who were not able to visit the holy places in person developed the pious custom of making a procession during which they paused to meditate upon the Passion. This developed into the popular devotion The Way of the Cross.

The one who presides at the celebration invites all present to meditate upon the passion of Christ.

First Station: JESUS IS CONDEMNED TO DEATH

℣. We adore you, Christ, and we bless you.
℟. Because by your cross you redeemed the world.

Pilate took water and washed his hands before the crowd, saying, I am innocent of this man's blood; see to it yourselves. And all the people answered, His blood be on us and on our children! Then having scourged Jesus, delivered him to be crucified.
(Mt 27, 24–26)

Our Father.

℣. Through the Passion of your Son,
℟. Pray for our salvation, O Virgin Mary.

Second Station: JESUS CARRIES THE CROSS

Jesus said to all, If anyone would come after me, let him deny himself and take up his cross daily and follow me. For whoever would save his life will lose it; and whoever loses his life for my sake, will save it.
(Lk 9, 23–24)

Third Station: JESUS FALLS THE FIRST TIME

Surely he has borne our griefs and carried our sorrows; yet we esteemed him stricken, smitten by God, and afflicted. But he was wounded for our transgressions, he was bruised for our iniquities; upon him was the chastisement that made us whole, and with his stripes we are healed.
(Is 53, 4–5)

Simeon said to Mary his mother, "Behold, this child is set for the fall and rising of many in Israel, and for a sign that is spoken against, and a sword will pierce through your own soul also. Mary kept all these things in her heart. (Lk 2, 34–35.51)

Fifth Station: JESUS IS HELPED BY SIMON THE CYRENIAN

As they led Jesus away, they seized one Simon of Cyrene, who was coming in from the country, and laid on him the cross, to carry it behind Jesus. (Lk 23, 26)

The Lord said to me "Seek my face". My heart says to you, "Your face, Lord, do I seek". Hide not your face from me. (Psalm 27, 8) Jesus said, "Who sees me sees him who sent me". (Jn 12, 45)

Seventh Station: JESUS FALLS THE SECOND TIME.

Jesus says: "Come to me, all who labour and are heavy laden, and I will give you rest. Take my yoke upon you, and learn from me; for I am gentle and lowly in heart, and you will find rest for your souls." (Mt 11, 28–29)

And there followed him a great multitude of the people, and of women who bewailed and lamented him. But Jesus turning to them said, "Daughters of Jerusalem, do not weep for me, but weep for yourselves and for your children." (Lk 23, 27–28)

Ninth Station: JESUS FALLS THE THIRD TIME

Look and see if there is any sorrow like my sorrow which was brought upon me. Their yoke was set upon my neck; he caused my strength to fail; he gave me into the hands of those whom I cannot withstand. (Lam 1, 12.14)

Tenth Station: JESUS IS STRIPPED OF HIS GARMENTS

When the soldiers had crucified Jesus they took his garments and made four parts, one for each soldier; also his tunic. But the tunic was without seam, woven from top to bottom. (Jn 19, 23)

Eleventh Station: JESUS IS NAILED TO THE CROSS

When they came to the place which is called The Skull, there they crucified him, and the criminals, one on the right and one on the left. And Jesus said, "Father, forgive them; for they know not what they do." (Lk 23, 33–34)

When Jesus saw his mother, and the disciple whom he loved standing near, he said to his mother, Woman, behold, your son! Then he said to the disciple, Behold, your mother! Then Jesus said, It is finished; and he bowed his head and gave up his spirit. (Jn 19, 26–27.30)

When the soldiers came to Jesus they did not break his legs. But one of the soldiers pierced his side with a spear, and at once there came out blood and water. After this Joseph of Arimathea, asked Pilate that he might take away the body of Jesus, and Pilate gave him leave. (Jn 19, 33–34.38)

Joseph took the body, and wrapped it in a clean linen shroud, and laid it in his own new tomb, which he had hewn in the rock; and he rolled a great stone to the door of the tomb, and departed. Mary Magdalene and the other Mary were there, sitting opposite the sepulchre. (Mt 27, 59–61)

Let us pray

Father, in every place
the salvation won by the sacrifice of Christ
is brought about through the preaching of the Gospel,
and your adopted children receive from Him the
    Word of truth,
the new life promised to all who believe in him.
Through Christ our Lord.

℟ Amen.

The Stations are the first representation of the Via Crucis, *as established by Saint Leonard of Porto Maurizio.*
Via Crucis, G. B. Tiepolo, San Polo, Venice

Via Lucis

As a complement to the Via Crucis, *there has arisen in recent times the devotion of the* Via Lucis: *meditation on the glorious mysteries of the Lord, namely, the events between the Resurrection and Pentecost. We learn to walk in the world as "children of the light", witnesses of the Risen Lord.*

The one who presides invites all present to meditate upon the resurrection of Christ.

First Station: JESUS RISES FROM THE DEAD

℣ We adore you, O Christ, and we bless you.
℟ Because by your Cross and Resurrection you have redeemed the world.

I know that you seek Jesus who was crucified. He is not here; for he has risen, as he said. Come, see the place where he lay. (Mt 28, 5–6)
As dawn breaks a mysterious face presents itself to the women who with sadness and love came early to the sepulchre of Jesus of Nazareth. It is the angel, the messenger of God, that reveals the glory of him who has passed beyond the frontier of death: the grave is open, Christ is risen and now lives for ever in heaven, where he awaits us.

Our Father.

℣ Through the resurrection of Christ,
℟ Keep us in the light, O Mother of the Lord.

Second Station: THE DISCIPLES FIND THE EMPTY SEPULCHRE

The disciple, who had reached the tomb first, entered, and he saw and believed (Jn 20, 8). Peter and the beloved disciple ran together that morning to the tomb of Jesus. The disciple sees only the winding cloth and a shroud. Yet not only does this cause surprise but through faith "he saw and believed" in the Lord, the one who had overcome death. All those who believe in Christ through faith see and believe.

Third Station: THE RISEN LORD APPEARS TO MARY MAGDALENE

Jesus said to her: "Mary!" She turned and said him: "Rabbuni", which means Master. (Jn 20, 16) Mary of Magdala, who had been in the company of Jesus for many months, who had listened to him and saw his hands stretched out to heal the sick, does not recognize him on Easter morning. It is necessary to be called by name as a personal vocation, because only the eyes of faith can see what the purely human gaze cannot understand.

"Was it not necessary that the Christ should suffer these things and enter into his glory?" And beginning with Moses and all the prophets, he interpreted to them in all the scriptures the things concerning himself. (Lk 24, 26–27). Two disciples are walking along the road that leads from Jerusalem to Emmaus and a stranger joins them. His words reveal a depth of meaning that has until now been hidden. Those who listen to those words will find that their hearts burn within them and bring hope and trust.

Fifth Station: THE RISEN LORD IS RECOGNIZED IN THE
BREAKING OF THE BREAD

As he sat at dinner with them, he took the bread and blessed it and broke it and gave it them. And their eyes were opened and they recognized him. (Lk 24, 30–31) It is evening. The two disciples of Emmaus have invited that · mysterious traveller to their table. He has explained to them the meaning of the events which they had lived through. After his words come his actions: he breaks the bread, the same gesture as at the Last Supper. That face becomes unexpectedly recognizable: he is still the Christ of the Upper Room, giving his body and blood as food for the life of the world.

Why are you troubled? And why do thoughts arise in your hearts? Look at my hands and my feet: It is I myself. (Lk 24, 38–39) At first they fear that they are seeing a ghost, for they still think that Jesus is buried in the tomb with the marks of his passion and crucifixion. But no, there he is, alive with the fullness of life, standing before his friends, with hands and feet bearing the marks of the wounds. This new life dispels the sadness, doubt and the sorrow and points to what lies beyond the silence of the grave.

Seventh Station: THE RISEN LORD GIVES THE POWER TO FORGIVE SINS

He breathed on them and said to them: "Receive the Holy Spirit; whose sins you shall forgive, they will be forgiven." (Jn 20, 22–23) Jesus breathes on his disciples as a sign of the life that is given to them. It is the sign of the regeneration that only the Holy Spirit can bring about in every individual through death to sin and new life in truth and justice. When this divine breath blows in the Church it brings about the renewal, transformation and sanctification of humanity.

Eighth Station: THE RISEN LORD STRENGTHENS
THE FAITH OF THOMAS

Jesus said to Thomas: "Be not faithless, but believing." Thomas answered: "My Lord and my God." (Jn 20, 27–28) Doubt had entered the heart of the disciple who had listened to Jesus and seen the signs of his divine power during his days on earth. Now the Risen Lord is there, standing before Thomas, truly risen from the dead. The disciple is enlightened and makes his firm profession of faith in the words "My Lord and my God".

Ninth Station: THE RISEN LORD APPEARS BY THE LAKE OF TIBERIAS

The disciple whom Jesus loved said to Peter: "It is the Lord!" Jesus then came, took bread and gave it them. (Jn 21, 7.13) Early in the morning there is a man standing on the shore of the lake of Tiberias. The disciples of Jesus had returned to their work as fishermen and were out in their boats. The beloved disciple looks at that figure on the shore and says: "It is the Lord!" Christ awaits them on the beach, ready to offer to the tired and uncertain men the bread of his presence.

"Simon, son of John, do you love me more than these?" He said to him: "Lord, you know that I love you." He said to him: "Feed my lambs." (Jn 21, 15)
Three questions and three answers of love form the heart of the dialogue between the risen Christ and Peter on the shore of the lake of Tiberias. The disciple who denied his master three times now professes three times his faith and love, and Christ gives him the mission to be the shepherd of his flock until the end of time. Through Peter, Christ will continue to lead his Church.

Eleventh Station: THE RISEN LORD SENDS OUT THE DISCIPLES INTO THE WHOLE WORLD

Go and teach all nations, baptizing them in the name of the Father, of the Son and of the Holy Spirit. I am with you always, till the end of the world. (Mt 28, 19–20)
On a mountain in Galilee, the glorious Christ of the resurrection greets his disciples. Though not visible, his presence will be real, effective and constant and he will always support the apostolic mission of the Church that proclaims the Gospel and gives the new life in the Spirit through the baptism.

Men of Galilee, why do you stand looking up to heaven? This Jesus, who is taken up from you into heaven, will come in the same manner as you have seen him go into heaven. (Acts 1,11) The Mount of Olives becomes the sign of the meeting of heaven and earth, accomplished in the risen Christ. He returns to his eternal glory to await the whole of redeemed humanity. But the believer must live in this world, proclaiming and establishing the Kingdom here while awaiting the return of Christ. "And we will always be with the Lord". (1 Thess 4, 17)

Thirteenth Station: AWAITING THE HOLY SPIRIT WITH THE BLESSED VIRGIN MARY

The apostles continued with one accord in prayer, with some women and Mary, the mother of Jesus, and with his disciples. (Acts 1, 14) The Christian community is gathered around Mary, one in faith, constant in prayer and in love. The Apostles and faithful followers of Jesus, men and women, with one voice praise God, testifying in love their faith in the risen Christ, awaiting the promise of Jesus to send the Consoling Spirit "who remains with you for ever" (Jn 14, 16).

Suddenly there came a sound from heaven, as of a rushing mighty wind. There appeared to them what looked like tongues of fire and they were filled with the Holy Spirit. (Acts 2, 2–4) In the Upper Room, on the day of Pentecost, came the wind of the Holy Spirit, that is the divine breath poured out on the disciples of the risen Christ. He lights the fire of the love that warms the hearts of believers and leads them in the world to testify to the life, the light and the love of God. The Church of countless languages, of different cultures and nationalities has in Jerusalem her roots and in the Holy Spirit her source.

Let us pray.

God our Father,
you give joy to the world,
by the resurrection of your Son, our Lord Jesus Christ.
Through the prayers of his mother, the Virgin Mary,
bring us to the happiness of eternal life.
Through Christ our Lord.

℟ Amen.

The icons have been painted especially for this book by Sister Anna Maria Di Domenico. They are in San Giovanni Rotondo.

The Rosary

The Rosary, through the repetition of the Hail Mary, leads us to contemplate the mysteries of the faith. This simple prayer, feeding the love of the Christian people for the Mother of God, illustrates the purpose of Marian prayer more clearly, namely, the glorification of Christ. (John Paul II, 5 November 1997)

JOYFUL MYSTERIES

1. The annunciation of the angel to Mary

The angel said to Mary: "Hail, full of grace, the Lord is with you. You will conceive a son, you will give birth to him and will call him Jesus." Mary said: "Here I am, I am the handmaid of the Lord." And the Word was made flesh and dwelt among us. (from Lk 1, 28. 31. 38; Jn 1, 14)

2. The visit of Mary to Elizabeth

Mary, entered the house of Zacharias and greeted Elizabeth. When Elizabeth heard the greeting of Mary, the babe leapt in her womb and, full of the Holy Spirit, she said: "Blessed are you among women and blessed is the fruit of your womb." (Lk 1, 40–42)

3. The birth of Jesus in Bethlehem

While Mary and Joseph were in Bethlehem, the days were accomplished that she should be delivered. She brought forth her firstborn son and wrapped him in swaddling clothes and laid him in a manger, because there was no room for them in the inn. (Lk 2, 6–7)

4. The presentation of Jesus in the temple

Mary and Joseph brought their son to Jerusalem, to present him to the Lord. Simeon blessed them and said to Mary, his mother: "This child is set for the fall and rising of many in Israel. And a sword shall pierce through your soul."
(Lk 2, 22.34–35)

5. The finding of Jesus in the temple

After three days, Mary and Joseph found Jesus in the temple. His mother said: "Son, why have you done this? Your father and I have looked for you anxiously." Jesus answered: "Why have you looked for me? Did you not know that I must be about my Father's business?"
(Lk 2, 46–48)

SORROWFUL MYSTERIES

1. The agony in the garden

When he came to the mount of Olives, Jesus knelt down and prayed: "Father, if you will, take this cup from me! Nevertheless, your will be done." Being in an agony he prayed more fervently and his sweat became as great drops of blood falling down to the ground. (Luke 22, 42.44)

2. The scourging at the pillar

Pilate said to them: "Whom do you want that I release to you: Barabbas or Jesus which is called Christ?" He knew well that they had delivered Jesus up out of envy. He released Barabbas and after having scourged Jesus, he delivered him to the soldiers to be crucified. (Mt 27, 17–18.26)

3. Jesus is crowned with thorns

The soldiers led Jesus into the hall called the Praetorium and they called together the whole band. They clothed him with purple, plaited a crown of thorns and put it on his head. They began to mock him, saying: "Hail, King of the Jews!" And they smote him on the head with a reed and spat upon him. (Mk 15, 16–19)

4. Jesus carries the cross to Calvary

After having mocked Jesus, the soldiers took off the purple garment from him and put his own clothes on him, then they led him out to crucify him. They brought him to the place called Golgotha, which means the place of a skull. (Mk 15, 20.22)

5. Jesus dies on the cross

Jesus, seeing his mother and the disciple whom he loved, said to his mother: "Woman, here is your son!" Then he said to the disciple: "Here is your mother!" After this, Jesus said: "I thirst". Having tasted the vinegar, he said: "It is finished!" And bowing his head, he gave up his spirit. (Jn 19, 26–30)

GLORIOUS MYSTERIES

1. The Resurrection: Jesus rises from the dead

Entering the sepulchre, the women saw a young man clothed in a white garment and they were afraid. And he said them: "Do not be afraid! You seek Jesus of Nazareth, the crucified. He is risen; he is not here." (Mk 16, 5–6)

2. Jesus ascends into heaven

Jesus was taken up and a cloud received him under the sight of the apostles. Two men in white apparel said to them: "This same Jesus, which is taken up from you into heaven, will come in like manner as you have seen him go into heaven." (Acts 1, 9–11)

3. The descent of the Holy Spirit at Pentecost

The apostles continued with one accord in prayer, with some women and Mary, the mother of Jesus. When the day of Pentecost was come, suddenly there came a sound from heaven as of a rushing mighty wind and there appeared to them tongues of fire; and they were all filled with the Holy Spirit. (Acts 1, 14; 2, 1–4)

4. The Assumption of the Blessed Virgin Mary into heaven

Mary said: "My soul magnifies the Lord and my spirit rejoices in God, my Saviour, because he regarded the low estate of his handmaiden. From now on all generations will call me blessed. The Almighty has done great things for me and holy is his name." (Lk 1, 46–49)

5. Mary is crowned as Queen of heaven

The temple of God in heaven was opened and there appeared in it the ark of the covenant. There appeared a great wonder in heaven: a woman clothed with the sun, and the moon under her feet and upon her head a crown of twelve stars. (Rev 11, 19 – 12, 1)

Salve Regina

*H*ail, holy Queen, Mother of mercy; hail, our life,
our sweetness and our hope.
To thee do we cry, poor banished children of Eve.
To thee do we send up our sighs,
mourning and weeping in this valley of tears.
Turn, then, most gracious advocate,
thine eyes of mercy toward us,
and after this, our exile, show unto us the
blessed fruit of thy womb, Jesus.
O clement, O loving, O sweet Virgin Mary.

*S*alve, Regina, mater misericordiæ,
vita, dulcedo et spes nostra, salve.
Ad te clamamus, exsules filii Eva.
Ad te suspiramus, gementes et flentes
in hac lacrimarum valle.
Eia ergo, advocata nostra,
illos tuos misericordes oculos ad nos converte.
Et Iesum, benedictum fructum ventris tui,
nobis post hoc exsilium ostende.
O clemens, o pia, o dulcis Virgo Maria.

Other prayers to Mary pp. 235–236.
Litany of the Blessed Virgin Mary p. 231.

The preceding images are based on the fifteen
mysteries of the Rosary surrounding the image of Our Lady
Shrine of Pompeii

Queen of Victory,
Glorious Queen of the Rosary,
we, your devoted children,
pour out the affections of our hearts to you.
VOTIVE BANNER OF THE LEGIONARIES FROM THE BATTLE OF LEPANTO,
Unknown Venetian, Basilica of San Vito dei Normanni, Brindisi

Texts for Common and Personal Prayer

The Jubilee pilgrimage is, first of all, a journey of prayer. Beyond the communal celebrations in the Roman Basilicas, there must be during the pilgrimage times of silence and of meditation. Texts are given for both common and private prayer.

TO THE HOLY TRINITY

The faith of all Christians is built on the Trinity
(St Caesarius of Arles)

Glory be to the Father and to the Son and to the Holy Spirit. As it was at the beginning, is now and ever shall be world without end. Amen.

Holy God, Holy power, Holy eternal, have mercy on us.

Let us bless the Father and the Son with the Holy Spirit, let us praise and extol him for ever.

God the Father, our creator, have pity on us.
God the Son, our redeemer, have pity on us.
God the Spirit, our sanctifier, have pity on us.
Holy Trinity, one God and Lord, have pity on us.

INVOCATIONS TO JESUS OUR SAVIOUR

Lord, have mercy.   *Lord, have mercy.*
Christ, have mercy.   *Christ, have mercy.*
Lord, have mercy.   *Lord, have mercy.*

Christ hear us.   *Christ graciously hear us.*
Christ hear our prayer.   *Christ hear our prayer.*

Jesus, beloved Son of the Father, divine knowledge, splendour of his glory.   ℟ *Have mercy on us.*

Jesus, son of Adam,
   descendant of Abraham,
   holy bud of David, ℟

Jesus, fulfilment of prophecy,
   fullness of the law, destiny of mankind, ℟

Jesus, gift of the Father,
   conceived by the working of the Spirit,
   son of the Virgin Mary, ℟

Jesus, born for our salvation,
   revealed to the shepherds, manifested to the Magi, ℟

Jesus, light of the people, glory of Israel, awaited by the
   nations, ℟

Jesus, baptized in the Jordan,
   consecrated by the Spirit, sent by the Father, ℟

Jesus, tried in the desert,
   praying on the mountain, glorious on Mount Tabor, ℟

Jesus, teacher of truth,
   word of life, way to the Father, ℟

Jesus, recovery of the sick,
   consolation of the afflicted,
   mercy for sinners, ℟

Jesus, way and door to salvation,
   shepherd and lamb, resurrection and life, ℟

Jesus, condemned to death,
   crowned with thorns, covered with sores, ℟

Jesus, nailed to the wood,
   buried in the earth, risen from the dead, ℟

Jesus, descended into hell,
   ascended into heaven, giver of the Spirit, ℟

Jesus, expected by the Bride,
   reward of the justified, fullness of the Kingdom, ℟

To you Jesus, the Living One, ℟ *Praise and glory.*
To you Jesus, living in the Church, ℟
To you Jesus, living for ever and ever, ℟

INVOCATIONS OF THE HOLY SPIRIT

Celestial king, Consoling Spirit, Spirit of Truth, that are present everywhere. Treasure of each good and Source of Life. Come, dwell in us, purify and save us, You that are Good!

(from Byzantine liturgy)

COME, Holy Spirit, Creator
blest, and in our souls take
up Thy rest; come with Thy
grace and heavenly aid to fill the
hearts which Thou hast made.

O comforter, to Thee we cry,
O heavenly gift of God Most High,
O fount of life and fire of love,
and sweet anointing from above.

Thou in Thy sevenfold gifts are known;
Thou, finger of God's hand we own;
Thou, promise of the Father, Thou
Who dost the tongue with
power imbue.

Kindle our senses from above,
and make our hearts o'erflow with love;
with patience firm and virtue high
the weakness of our flesh supply.

Far from us drive the foe we dread,
and grant us Thy peace instead;
so shall we not, with Thee for guide,
turn from the path of life aside.

Oh, may Thy grace on us bestow
the Father and the Son to know;
and Thee, through endless
    times confessed,
of both the eternal Spirit blest.

Now to the Father and the Son,
Who rose from death, be glory given,
with Thou, O Holy Comforter,
henceforth by all in earth and heaven.
Amen.

Veni, Creator Spiritus,
mentes tuorum visita,
imple superna gratia
quae tu creasti pectora.

Qui diceris Paraclitus,
altissima donum Dei,
fons vivus, ignis, caritas,
et spiritalis unctio.

Tu, septiformis munere,
digitus paternae dexterae,
Tu rite promissum Patris,
sermone ditans guttura.

Accende lumen sensibus:
infunde amorem cordibus:
infirma nostri corporis
virtute firmans perpeti.

Hostem repellas longius,
pacemque dones protinus:
ductore sic te praevio
vitemus omne noxium.

Per te sciamus da Patrem,
noscamus atque Filium;
Teque utriusque Spiritum
credamus omni tempore.

Deo Patri sit gloria,
et Filio, qui a mortuis
surrexit, ac Paraclito,
in saeculorum saecula.
Amen.

LITANY OF THE SAINTS

On her way the pilgrim Church experiences her bond with the Saints. The litany is the invocation of divine help, which we trust to the prayers of these models of life.

I. Supplications to God

Lord, have mercy on us.   *Lord, have mercy on us.*
Christ, have mercy on us. *Christ, have mercy on us.*
Lord, have mercy on us.   *Lord, have mercy on us.*

II. Invocation of the Saints

Kidame Mebret
Cathedral of Asmara,
Eritrea

Holy Mary,   *pray for us.*
Holy Mother of God,   *pray for us.*
Holy Virgin of Virgins,   *pray for us.*
Sts Michael, Gabriel and Raphael,
                    pray for us.

All Holy Angels and Archangels,
                    pray for us.

All Holy Orders of Blessed Spirits,
                    pray for us.

St John the Baptist,   *pray for us.*
St Joseph,   *pray for us.*

All Holy Patriarchs and Prophets,
                    pray for us.

Saint James
Shrine of
Compostela, Spain

St Peter,   *pray for us.*
St Paul,   *pray for us.*
St Andrew,   *pray for us.*
St James,   *pray for us.*
St John,   *pray for us.*
St Thomas,   *pray for us.*
St James,   *pray for us.*
St Philip,   *pray for us.*

Saint Maria Goretti
Shrine of Nettuno,
Italy

Saint Augustine
Shrine of Tolentino,
Italy

St Bartholomew, *pray for us.*
St Matthew, *pray for us.*
St Simon, *pray for us.*
St Thaddeus, *pray for us.*
St Barnabas, *pray for us.*
St Luke, *pray for us.*
St Mark, *pray for us.*

All Holy Apostles and Evangelists,
pray for us.

All Holy Disciples of our Lord,
pray for us.

All Holy Innocents, *pray for us.*

St Stephen, *pray for us.*
St Lawrence, *pray for us.*
St Vincent, *pray for us.*
Sts Fabian and Sebastian,
pray for us.
Sts John and Paul, *pray for us.*
Sts Cosmas and Damian,
pray for us.
Sts Gervase and Protasius,
pray for us.

All Holy Martyrs, *pray for us.*

St Sylvester, *pray for us.*
St Gregory, *pray for us.*
St Ambrose, *pray for us.*
St Augustine, *pray for us.*
St Jerome, *pray for us.*
St Martin, *pray for us.*
St Nicholas, *pray for us.*

Saint Benedict
Shrine of Subbiaco,
Italy

All Holy Bishops and Confessors,
pray for us.

All Holy Doctors, *pray for us.*

St Anthony, *pray for us.*
St Benedict, *pray for us.*
St Bernard, *pray for us.*
St Dominic, *pray for us.*
St Francis, *pray for us.*

All Holy Priests and Levites,
pray for us.

All Holy Monks and Hermits,
pray for us.

St Mary Magdalen, *pray for us.*
St Agatha, *pray for us.*
St Lucy, *pray for us.*
St Agnes, *pray for us.*
St Cecilia, *pray for us.*
St Catherine, *pray for us.*
St Anastasia, *pray for us.*

All Holy Virgins and Widows,
pray for us.

All Men and Women, Saints of God,
make intercession for us.

Saint Teresa of Avila
Church of Santa Maria
delle Vittorie, Italy

III. Invocations to Christ

Christ, Son of the living God   ℟ *Have mercy on us.*
You who came into this world, ℟
You who were crucified for our sake, ℟
You who gave yourself to death for us, ℟
You who lay in the sepulchre, ℟
You who went down into hell, ℟
You who rose from the dead, ℟
You who ascended to heaven, ℟
You who sent your Spirit on the Apostles, ℟
You who sit at the right hand of the Father, ℟
You who will come to judge the living and the dead, ℟

IV. Supplications for different needs

Grant us your mercy.   ℟ *Hear us, Lord.*
Raise our hearts to desire heaven. ℟
Save us with all our brothers from everlasting death. ℟
Free the human race from hunger, war and every sorrow. ℟
Give the whole world justice and peace. ℟
Comfort and enlighten your holy Church. ℟
Bless the Pope, the bishops, clergy and all ministers of
    the Gospel. ℟
Send new workers to your harvest. ℟
Give all Christians unity in the faith. ℟
Lead all men to the truth. ℟

(these may be added)

Look after our Church N. with its bishop N. ℟
Be present in every home and in every family. ℟
Support and comfort the old with your grace. ℟
Help the young to grow in your friendship. ℟
Enlighten governments and rulers with knowledge of you. ℟
Defend those persecuted in the cause of justice. ℟
Bring exiles home. ℟
Comfort all who are sick and suffering. ℟
Bring the departed to the joy of your kingdom. ℟

Conclusion

Christ, hear our prayer. Christ, grant our supplication.

LITANY OF THE BLESSED VIRGIN MARY

The Litany of Loreto *is a collection of the names given to Mary.*

Shrine of Loreto,
Italy

Shrine of Lourdes,
France

Lord, have mercy. *Lord have mercy.*
Christ have mercy.

Christ have mercy.

Lord have mercy. *Lord have mercy.*
Holy Mary, *pray for us.*
Holy Mother of God, *pray for us.*
Holy Virgin of Virgins, *pray for us.*
Mother of Christ, *pray for us.*
Mother of divine grace, *pray for us.*
Mother most pure, *pray for us.*
Mother most chaste, *pray for us.*
Mother inviolate, *pray for us.*
Mother undefiled, *pray for us.*
Mother most amiable, *pray for us.*
Mother most admirable, *pray for us.*
Mother of good Counsel, *pray for us.*
Mother of our Creator, *pray for us.*
Mother of our Saviour, *pray for us.*
Virgin most prudent, *pray for us.*
Virgin most venerable, *pray for us.*
Virgin most renowned, *pray for us.*
Virgin most powerful, *pray for us.*
Virgin most merciful, *pray for us.*
Virgin most faithful, *pray for us.*
Mirror of justice, *pray for us.*
Seat of wisdom, *pray for us.*
Cause of our joy, *pray for us.*
Spiritual vessel, *pray for us.*
Vessel of honour, *pray for us.*
Singular vessel of devotion, *pray for us.*
Mystical rose, *pray for us.*
Tower of David, *pray for us.*
Tower of ivory, *pray for us.*
House of gold, *pray for us.*
Ark of the covenant, *pray for us.*

Shrine of Fatima,
Portugal

Gate of heaven, *pray for us.*
Morning star, *pray for us.*
Health of the sick, *pray for us.*
Refuge of sinners, *pray for us.*
Comforter of the afflicted, *pray for us.*
Help of Christians, *pray for us.*
Queen of Angels, *pray for us.*
Queen of Patriarchs, *pray for us.*
Queen of Prophets, *pray for us.*
Queen of Apostles, *pray for us.*
Queen of Martyrs, *pray for us.*
Queen of Confessors, *pray for us.*
Queen of Virgins, *pray for us.*
Queen of all Saints, *pray for us.*
Queen conceived without
    original sin, *pray for us.*
Queen assumed into heaven,
pray for us.
Queen of the most holy Rosary,
pray for us.
Queen of families, *pray for us.*
Queen of peace, *pray for us.*

Lamb of God, who takest away the sins of the world,
Spare us, O Lord.

Lamb of God, who takest away the sins of the world,
Graciously hear us, O Lord.

Lamb of God, who takest away the sins of the world,
Have mercy on us.

If the Litany ends with the Rosary:

God of infinite wisdom, you chose the Blessed Virgin Mary, outstanding among the humble and poor of Israel, to be the Mother of the Saviour; may we welcome your word with living faith and learn to place our hope for salvation only in you. We ask this through Christ our Lord.

℟ Amen.

Shrine of
Czestochowa,
Poland

Shrine of Guadalupe,
Mexico

ANGELUS

The angel of the Lord
declared unto Mary.
And she conceived by the
Holy Spirit.

Hail, Mary.

Behold the handmaid of the
Lord.
Be it done unto me according
to thy word.

Hail, Mary.

And the Word was made flesh.
And dwelt among us.

Hail, Mary.

℣. Pray for us,
O Holy Mother of God.

℟. That we may be made
worthy of the promises of
Christ.

Let us pray

Pour forth, we beseech
Thee, O Lord, Thy grace
into our hearts, that we to
whom the incarnation of
Christ, Thy Son, was made
known by the message of an
angel, may by His passion and
cross be brought to the glory
of His resurrection, through
the same Christ our Lord.

℟. Amen.

Shrine of
Washington, DC,USA

REGINA CAELI

(Easter time)

O Queen of heaven, rejoice,
   alleluia;
For He Whom you merited to
   bear, alleluia,

Has risen as he said, alleluia:
Pray for us to God, alleluia.

℣. Rejoice and be glad, O
   Virgin Mary, alleluia.
℟. For the Lord is truly risen,
   alleluia.

Let us pray

O God, Who by the
   resurrection of your Son,
our Lord Jesus Christ,
has given joy to the whole
   world,
grant, we beseech you, that
through the intercession of the
Blessed Virgin Mary, His mother,
we may attain the joys of
   eternal life,
through the same Christ our
   Lord.
℟. Amen.

Shrine of Shanghai,
China

IN HONOUR OF THE MOTHER OF THE LORD

Along with the Hail Mary the Church has other venerable prayers of praise and of supplication to the Mother of God.

Hail, Mary, full of grace; the Lord is with thee; blessed art thou among women, and blessed is the fruit of thy womb, Jesus. * Holy Mary, Mother of God, pray for us sinners, now and at the hour of our death. Amen.

Holy Mother of the Saviour, door of the heavens, star of the sea, support your people panting to rise up. You who greeted the welcome of the angel, to the amazement of all creation, and gave birth to your Creator, Mother ever virgin, have pity on us sinners.

Hail, Queen of the heavens, hail, lady of the angels; door and root of salvation, you bring light into the world. Rejoice, glorious virgin, beautiful among all women; hail, all holy one, pray to Christ the Lord for us.

Shrine of Our Lady Aparecida (Brazil)

Shrine of Antipolo, Philippines

235

Shrine of Mariazell,
Austria

Shrine of Lujan,
Argentina

We turn to you for
protection,
holy Mother of God.
Listen to our prayers
and help us in our needs.
Save us from every danger,
glorious and blessed Virgin.

Glorious ever virgin and
blessed Mother of God,
present our prayer to your
Son, our God: ask him, for
your sake, to save our souls!

(from the Byzantine liturgy)

Mother of God, you are the
true vine that brought
forth the Fruit of life. We
implore you, O Blessed Lady:
with the Apostles and all
Saints, intercede that Christ
may have pity on our souls.

(from the Byzantine liturgy)

Hail, Holy Queen *p. 222.*

My soul glorifies the Lord
p. 172.

SPECIAL INTENTIONS

For the Pope
Let us pray for our holy father Pope N.,
that the Lord, who has chosen him, grant him life
and health and preserve him to his holy Church.

Father of providence, look with love on N. our
Pope, your appointed successor to Saint Peter
on whom you built your Church. May he be the
visible centre and foundation of our unity in faith
and love. Grant this through our Lord Jesus Christ,
your Son, who lives and reigns with you and the
Holy Spirit, one God, for ever and ever.

For the Bishop
Let us pray for our Bishop N.,
that the Lord may grant him to carry out faithfully
the office of teacher, priest and shepherd.

God, our Father, our shepherd and guide, look with
love on N. your servant, your appointed pastor of
the Church. May his word and example inspire and
guide the Church; may he, and all those in his care,
come to the joy of everlasting life. Grant this through ...

For the ministers of the Church

Father, you have taught the ministers of your
Church not to desire that they be served but to
serve their brothers and sisters. May they be
effective in their work and persevering in their
prayer, performing their ministry with gentleness
and concern for others. We ask this through ...

For the laity

God our Father, you send the power of the Gospel
into the world as a life-giving leaven. Fill with
the Spirit of Christ those whom you call to live in the
midst of the world and its concerns; help them by
their work on earth to build up your eternal
kingdom. We ask this through ...

Shrine of Saint Anthony of
Padua, Italy

For religious vocations

Father, you call all who believe in you to grow perfect in love by following in the footsteps of Christ your Son. May those whom you have chosen to serve you as religious provide by their way of life a convincing sign of your kingdom for the Church and the whole world. We ask this through ...

For those who serve in public office

Almighty and eternal God, you know the longings of men's hearts and you protect their rights. In your goodness, watch over those in authority, so that people everywhere may enjoy freedom, security, and peace. We ask this through ...

For the family

Father, we look to your loving guidance and order as the pattern of all family life. By following the example of the holy family of your Son, in mutual love and respect, may we come to the joy of our home in heaven. We ask this through ...

Saint Teresa of the Child Jesus
Shrine of Lisieux, France

For the spread of the Gospel

Father, you will your Church to be the sacrament of salvation for all peoples. Make us feel more urgently the call to work for the salvation of all men, until you have made us all one people. Inspire the hearts of all your people to continue the saving work of Christ everywhere until the end of the world. Grant this through ...

Prayer for peace

God our Father, creator of the world, you establish the order which governs all the ages. Hear our prayer and give us peace in our time that we may rejoice in your mercy and praise you without end. We ask this through ...

For those who do not believe in God

Almighty and eternal God you created mankind so that all might long to find you and have peace when you are found. Grant that, in spite of the hurtful things that stand in their way, they may all recognize in the lives of Christians the tokens of your love and mercy, and gladly acknowledge you as the one true God and Father of us all. We ask this through Christ our Lord.

Shrine of Medinaceli, Spain

For persecuted Christians

Father, in your mysterious providence, your Church must share in the sufferings of Christ your Son. Give the spirit of patience and love to those who are persecuted for their faith in you that they may always be true and faithful witnesses to your promise of eternal life. We ask this through ...

For unity of Christians

Almighty and eternal God, you keep together those you have united. Look kindly on all who follow Jesus your Son. We are all consecrated to you by our common baptism; make us one in the fullness of faith and keep us one in the fellowship of love. We ask this through ...

For people of other faiths

Almighty and eternal God, enable those who do not acknowledge Christ to find the truth as they walk before you in sincerity of heart. Help us to grow in love for one another, to grasp more fully the mystery of your godhead, and to become more perfect witnesses of your love in the sight of men. We ask this through Christ our Lord.

Padre Pio
Shrine of San Giovanni Rotondo, Italy

For the sick

Father, your Son accepted our sufferings to teach us the virtue of patience in human illness. Hear the prayers we offer for our sick brothers and sisters. May all who suffer pain, illness or disease realize that they are chosen to be saints, and know that they are joined to Christ in his suffering for the salvation of the world, who lives and reigns with you and the Holy Spirit, one God, for ever and ever.

For the suffering

Almighty, ever-living God, you give strength to the weary and new courage to those who have lost heart. Hear the prayers of all who call on you in any trouble that they may have the joy of receiving your help in their need. We ask this through Christ our Lord.

In thanksgiving

Father of mercy, you always answer your people in their sufferings. We thank you for your kindness and ask you to free us from all evil, that we may serve you in happiness all our days. We ask this through ...

Latin Hymns

HYMNS

Christus vincit

℟. *Christus vincit!*
Christus regnat!
Christus, Christus imperat!

N. Summo Pontifici
et universali patri,
pax, vita et salus perpetua! ℟.

N. reverendissimo Episcopo
et universo clero ac populo
ei commisso
pax, vita et salus perpetua! ℟.

Tempora bona veniant!
Pax Christi veniat!
Regnum Christi veniat! ℟.

Te Deum

Te Deum laudámus: *
te Dóminum confitémur.

Te ætérnum Patrem, *
omnis terra venerátur.

Tibi omnes angeli, *
tibi cæli et univérsæ potestates:

tibi chérubim et séraphim *
incessábili voce proclámant:

Sanctus, * Sanctus, *
Sanctus Dóminus Deus Sábaoth.

Pleni sunt cæli et terra *
maiestátis glóriæ tuæ.

Te gloriósus *
Apostolórum chorus,

te prophetárum *
laudábilis númerus,

te mártyrum candidátus *
laudat exércitus.

Te per orbem terrárum *
sancta confitétur Ecclésia,

Patrem * imménsæ maiestátis;

venerándum tuum verum *
et únicum Fílium;

Sanctum quoque *
Paráclitum Spíritum.

Tu rex glóriæ, * Christe.

Tu Patris * sempitérnus es Fílius.

Tu, ad liberándum
susceptúrus hóminem, *
non horruísti Vírginis úterum.

Tu, devícto mortis acúleo, *
aperuísti credéntibus regna
cælórum.

Tu ad déxteram Dei sedes, *
in glória Patris.

Iudex créderis * esse ventúrus.

Te ergo, quǽsumus,
tuis fámulis súbveni, *
quos pretióso sánguine
redemísti.

Ætérna fac cum sanctis tuis *
in glória numerári.

Ubi caritas

℟ *Ubi cáritas est vera,*
Deus ibi est.

Congregávit nos in unum
Christi amor.
Exsultémus et in ipso
iucundémur.
Timeámus et amémus
Deum vivum.
Et ex corde diligámus
nos sincéro. ℟

Simul ergo cum in unum
congregámur:
Ne nos mente dividámur,
caveámus.
Cessent iúrgia malígna,
cessent lites.
Et in médio nostri sit
Christus Deus. ℟

Simul quoque cum beátis
videámus
Gloriánter vultum tuum,
Christe Deus:
Gáudium, quod est imménsum
atque probum,
Sǽcula per infiníta sæculórum. ℟

Veni Creator *(see p. 226)*

Eucharistic Hymns

Adoro devote

Adóro devóte, latens véritas,
te quæ sub his formis
vere látitas:
tibi se cor meum totum súbicit,
quia te contémplans
totum déficit.

Visus, gustus, tactus,
in te fállitur;
sed solus audítus tute créditur.
Credo quicquid dixit
Dei Fílius:
nihil Veritátis verbo vérius.

In cruce latébat sola Déitas;
sed hic latet simul et humánitas.
Ambo tamen credens
atque cónfitens
peto quod petívit
latro pǽnitens.

Plagas, sicut Thomas,
non intúeor;
meum tamen Deum
te confíteor.
Fac me tibi semper
magis crédere,
in te spem habére, te dilígere.

O memoriále mortis Dómini,
Panis veram vitam
præstans hómini,
præsta meæ menti
de te vívere,
et te semper illi dulce sápere.

Pie pelicáne, Iesu Dómine,
me immúndum munda
tuo sánguine,
cuius una stilla salvum fácere
totum mundum posset
omni scélere.

Iesu, quem velátum
nunc aspício,
quando fiet illud
quod tam cúpio
ut, te reveláta cernens fácie,
visu sim beátus tuæ glóriæ?
                              Amen.

Ave verum

Ave verum Corpus natum
de Maria Virgine:
vere passum, immolatum
in cruce pro homine.

Cuius latus perforatum
fluxit aqua et sanguine:
esto nobis prægustatum
mortis in examine.

O Iesu dulcis! O Iesu pie!
O Iesu, fili Mariæ.

Ecce panis

Ecce panis angelórum,
factus cibus viatórum:
vere panis filiórum,
non mitténdus cánibus.

In figúris praesignátur,
cum Isaac immolátur,
Agnus Paschae deputátur,
datur manna pátribus.

Bone Pastor, panis vere,
Iesu, nostri miserére:
tu nos pasce, nos tuére,
tu nos bona fac vidére
in terra viventium.

Tu, qui cuncta scis et vales,
qui nos pascis hic mortales:
tuos ibi commensáles,
coheredes et sodáles
fac sanctórum cívium. Amen.

O salutaris hostia

O salutáris hóstia,
Quæ cæli pandis óstium,
Bella premunt hostília:
Da robur, fer auxílium.

Uni trinóque Dómino
Sit sempitérna glória,
Qui vitam sine término
Nobis donet in pátria. Amen.

Tantum ergo

Tantum ergo sacraméntum
venerémur cérnui,
et antíquum documéntum
novo cedat rítui;
præstet fides supplémentum
sénsuum deféctui.

Genitóri Genitóque
laus et iubilátio,
salus, honor, virtus quoque
sit et benedíctio;
procedénti ab utróque
compar sit laudátio. Amen.

Hymns and Prayers

Attende Domine

Atténde, Dómine,
et miserére,
quia peccávimus tibi.

Parce Domine

Parce Dómine,
parce pópulo tuo:
ne in ætérnum
irascáris nobis.

Lauda Ierusalem

Lauda Ierusalem Dominum
Lauda Deum tuum, Sion.
Hosanna, Hosanna,
Hosanna filio David.

Tu es Petrus

Tu es Petrus,
et super hanc petram
ædificábo Ecclésiam meam.

MARIAN HYMNS

Ave, maris stella

Ave, maris stella,
Dei mater alma
atque semper virgo
felix cæli porta.

Sumens illud "Ave"
Gabriélis ore,
funda nos in pace,
mutans Evæ nomen.

Solve vincla reis,
profer numen cæcis,
mala nostra pelle,
bona cuncta posce.

Monstra te esse matrem
sumat per te precem
qui pro nobis natus
tulit esse tuus.

Virgo singuláris,
inter omnis mitis,
nos culpis solútos
mites fac et castos.

Vitam præsta puram,
iter para tutum,
ut vidéntes Iesum
semper collætémur.

Sit laus Deo Patri,
summo Christo decus.
Spirítui Sancto
honor, tribus unus. Amen.

Magnificat

Magnificat*
ánima mea Dóminum.

Et exsultávit spíritus meus*
in Deo salvatore meo.

Quia respexit humilitáte
ancillæ suæ*.
Ecce enim ex hoc béatam me
dicent omnes generatiónes.

Quia fecit mihi magna,
qui potens est*,
et sanctum nomen eius,

Et misericordia eius
in progénies et progénies*
timéntibus eum.

Fecit poténtiam in bráchio suo,*
dispérsit supérbos mente
cordis sui;

Depósuit poténtes de sede*
et exaltávit húmiles;

Esuriéntes implévit bonis*
et dívites dimísit inánes.

Suscépit Israel púerum suum,*
recordátus misericórdiæ,

Sicut lócutus est ad patres
nostros,*
Abraham et sémini eius
in sǽcula.

Glória Patri. Sicut erat.

Salve Regina *(see p. 222)*

TEXTS AND PRAYERS

LATIN PRAYERS AND HYMNS

Hymns

Eucharistic hymns

Marian hymns

Other hymns and prayers

BIBLICAL REFERENCES

Psalms

Readings

The Continuum Publishing Company
370 Lexington Avenue, New York, NY10017

Original Italian edition © 1999 Arnoldo Mondadori S.p.A., Milan
Fabio Ratti Editoria S.r.l.

English translation © Geoffrey Chapman

Sections I and II translation by the Vatican; for help with the English language
texts of Section III the publishers thank Cuthbert Johnson OSB, Abbot of Quarr,
and Martin Foster of the Bishops' Conference Liturgy Office, London.

Library of Congress Cataloging-in-Publication Data
Pellegrini in preghiera nel giubileo dell'anno santo del 2000. English.
Pilgrim Prayers: the Official Vatican prayerbook for the Jubilee Year 2000 /
prepared by the Vatican Committee for the Jubilee Year 2000.
Includes index.
ISBN 0-8264-1186-X
1. Pilgrims and pilgrimages—Italy—Rome. 2. Holy Year, 2000 Prayer-books and
devotions—English. 3. Christian pilgrims and pilgrimages Prayer-books and devotions—English. I. Vatican City. Comitato centrale del grande giubileo dell'anno
duemila.   II. Title. BX2320.5.I8P4413 2000
242'.802—dc21   99-29243
                                                      CIP

Editorial consultancy Vito Mancuso

EDITORIAL
Barbara Cacciani, Giorgia Conversi,
Emanuela Damiani, Giovanni Francesio,
Laura Recordati, Silvia Scamperle

GRAPHIC DESIGN
Stefania Testa, Silvia Tomasone

PHOTOGRAPHS
Image Bank
Archivio Mondadori
Biblioteca Apostolica Vaticana

Typeset by Carr Studios
Printed in Spain
D.L. TO: 1810 - 1999

HYMN
for the celebration of the Great Jubilee of the year 2000

CHRIST TODAY, CHRIST YESTERDAY

Christ today, Christ yesterday,
Christ who was and is to come.
You are God and you are love
And you call us here today.

1. Blessed be God, Lord of all time.
Christ who proclaims the Jubilee:
offers to sinners joy and grace.
Praise, oh praise Him! Sing Gloria!
Amen! Alleluia!

2. Blessed be God! Let's follow Christ!
He pardons us of all our sins;
Seventy seven times forgiv'n.
Praise, oh praise Him! Sing Gloria!
Amen! Alleluia!

3. Blessed be God, the Word made flesh
Who for our sins was put to death,
death on a Cross at Golgotha.
Praise, oh praise Him! Sing Gloria!
Amen! Alleluia!

4. Blessed be God, the Holy Child,
Bethlehem's Infant, meek and mild,
born of a Virgin pure of heart.
Praise, oh praise Him! Sing Gloria!
Amen! Alleluia!

5. Blessed be God, the First-born Son,
Light in the dark, his brightness shone;
lowly He worked in Nazareth.
Praise, oh praise Him! Sing Gloria!
Amen! Alleluia!